The Golden Years and **The**

This volume brings togethe[...]
Miller, previously unpublishe[...]

The Golden Years is an historical tragedy about Montezuma's destruction at the hands of Cortez. Unable to convert the Aztecs, Cortez assumes the role of barbarian, ravager of a civilization. While Montezuma, as Miller has written, 'convinced himself that the strange white creatures who came out of the ocean were fated to be his masters and at the same time apotheosize him to godhood now that he had, as he believed, led his Aztecs to the conquest of all the known world.'

Written in 1940, *The Golden Years* remained unperformed for many years. It was presented as a radio play by BBC Radio 3 in 1987.

The Man Who Had All The Luck was first staged in 1944. In this fable about human freedom and individual responsibility the hero, David Beeves, acts out an ironic reversal of Job's plight. Plagued by the contrast between his own success and the failures of those around him, he tries to make sense of his good fortune. In doing so, David poignantly confronts the question of the justice of fate.

Arthur Miller

The Golden Years
and
The Man Who Had all the Luck

With an Introduction by the author

and an Afterword by Christopher Bigsby

METHUEN DRAMA

First published in Great Britain in 1989 simultaneously in hardback and paperback by Methuen Drama, Michelin House, 81 Fulham Rd, London SW3 6RB

British Library Cataloguing in Publication Data
Miller, Arthur, 1915–
  Early plays.
  I. Title II. Miller, Arthur, 1915–. Golden years.
  III. Miller, Arthur, 1915–. Man who had all the luck
812' .52

ISBN 0–413–61660

Printed in Great Britain by Richard Clay Ltd, Bungay, Suffolk

Poem by William Butler Yeats reproduced on page 15 by kind permission of Messrs AP Watt.

The front cover shows an illustration of Cortez meeting Montezuma, reproduced by courtesy of the Mary Evans Picture Library, together with a photograph of a Marmon car, repoduced by courtesy of the National Motor Museum at Beaulieu. The photograph of Arthur Miller on the back cover is © Dan Weiner.

Introduction

Both of these plays came out of the years leading up to World War II, between 1938, my college graduation year, and 1944 when the fighting was raging. For me they are a kind of unadulterated evidence of my reactions to that time and it strikes me oddly that, as up to my neck as I was in the feverish anti-Fascism that swept my generation, the plays I chose to write were so metaphorical. This is especially strange when the only tradition in American theatre of which I was aware was realism. I can't imagine what I thought I was doing.

Or, rather, I thought I knew that I was writing against the grain of the Broadway theatre of the time, the only theatre we had, which as usual was happily wallowing in its traditional sidewalk realism. My primary argument with this form was that I could not connect aspiration with it – it was too much like uninterpreted life. *The Golden Years* looked toward a non-existent poetic theatre inspired by the Elizabethan models. Its lavish use of actors was no doubt encouraged by the fact that in the early months of its writing I was on the payroll, at $22.77 a week, of the expiring Playwriting Project of the WPA Theatre, and at least in theory could call upon any number of actors for my cast. Unfortunately, before the play was finished Congress had wiped out the WPA Theatre and the play, like any play calling for several immense sets and a cast so large, was doomed as a possible commercial enterprise. It was never produced until the BBC did a radio production in 1987.

Excepting for a revision of three pages at the end of *The Man Who Had All The Luck*, and some mild pruning of both plays, I have left them as they were. *The Man Who Had All The Luck* was given a regular Broadway production and lasted less than a full week after the critics, with one or two interested but puzzled exceptions, could make absolutely nothing of it. I recall at the time being unable to find the slightest connection between the production and the play I imagined I had written, and after watching but one bewildering performance fled back to my desk and began a novel, resolved never to write for the theatre again. It was forty-five years later, in 1988, that I began to understand the reason for my alienation from my own play, as well, very possibly, for the total incomprehension of the critics.

A staged reading of the play under the direction of Ralph Bell, an old friend who had always had a soft spot in his heart for this play, quickly revealed that it is, indeed, a fable with no relation to realistic theatre. A fable, of course, is based on an obsessive grip of a single idea bordering on the supernatural and it is the idea that stands in the forefront rather than the characters and the verisimilitudes of the tale. The coincidences are arrantly unapologetic in this play and so they should be played, rather than attempts made to rationalize them and dim them down.

I recall the original production lit in reassuring pink and rose, a small-town genre comedy. Given the threatening elements in the story this atmosphere must indeed have been puzzling. The play is after all attacking the evaluation of people by their success or failure and worse yet, denying the efficacy of property as a shield against psychological catastrophe.

From a distance of half a century I am struck by a certain optimistic undercurrent in both plays, despite one being a tragedy and the other veering pretty close. I must say that at the time, life at best seemed headed for a bloody showdown with Fascism, or at worst a hapless surrender to it, but while there is plenty of worry in these plays there is no real despair or defeat of the spirit. This will strike some as perhaps a reflection of a callow Leftism but in truth it was the way most Americans felt even after a very long decade of Depression. By the late Thirties and early Forties we had, of course, known much social violence and all kinds of vileness, but not yet a Holocaust, not yet the bursting of the banks of evil. I can still recall my incredulity at the daylight bombing of Guernica in the Spanish Civil War. As bombings go it wasn't a very big one. The big ones were still on the way. But I simply could not believe that a European flying low in an airplane on a sunny day over an undefended town, could, whatever his politics, drop live bombs on women out shopping with their baby carriages, on old men sitting before their doorways, on young lovers strolling across the ancient square! It was hard to sleep for weeks afterwards. It was still possible to be shocked. At least within one's mind the lines of some sort of order of permissible human behaviour still held.

In the West since the War of 1914–18 every period has known its main menace, some single force threatening life on the planet. For a long time now it has been Communism, and as this menace disintegrates there are signs that ecological catastrophe is developing into a world-wide substitute. From the mid-Thirties to the outbreak of war with the Axis powers it was the Fascist threat – and for some its promise – that pervaded every discussion. An important source of the energy in these plays was my fear that in one form or another Fascism, with its intensely organized energies, might well overwhelm the wayward and self-fixated Democracies. A reader today may find it strange that two such very different works could spring from the same source, or even, perhaps, that they are at all related to contemporaneous political events.

The tell-tale mark of this preoccupation, as I now see quite clearly, is much the same in both plays, even if one is a tragedy about the Cortez invasion of Montezuma's Mexico in 1522 and the other the tale of a very successful young man in a pastoral Ohio village. They are both struggling against passive acceptance of fate or even of defeat in life, and urge action to control one's future; both see evil as irrational and aggressive, the good as rational, if inactive and benign. Plainly, I was hounded at the time by what seemed the debility of Americans' grasp of democratic values or their awareness of them. And I must recall – to fill out this picture – that these plays were written after a decade of Depression, which had by no means lifted with any certainty as yet, and that the Depression had humbled us, shown us up as helpless before the persistent, ineradicable plague of mass unemployment. Reason had lost a lot of her credentials between 1930 and 1940.

`   If as the decade ended, the devaluation of the individual – the main lesson of the Depression – was still spiked to the common consciousness, these plays are somewhat surprising testimony to me that I had not lost the belief in the centrality of the individual and the importance of what he thought and did. On this evidence I suppose I might even have been called an individualist – there is nothing like writing a play for unveiling one's illusions! *The Man Who Had All The Luck* tells me that in the midst of the collectivist Thirties I believed it decisive what an individual thinks and does about his life, regardless of overwhelming social forces. And likewise, in *The Golden Years*, the fate of all Mexico hung on what an individual – Montezuma – believed about himself and his role in the universe. Indeed, if these plays are to be credited there is no force so powerful, politically as well as personally, as a man's self-conceptions.

Hearing *The Man Who Had All The Luck* read after four decades, it only then occurred to me that I had written the obverse of the Book of Job. The story of a man who cannot come to terms with the total destruction of his property and all his hopes, when he has done nothing to earn such treatment from God or fate, is very much the same as that of a man who can't seem to make a mistake and whose every move turns out to be profitable and good. What had Job done to deserve such disasters? David Beeves has much the same question in mind, oppressed by his invariably good luck in everything he attempts. And he projects an imminent disaster that will even things up between himself and the rest of humanity. For both these characters the menace is much the same – anarchy in the high command of the universe, a yawning breach between effect and conceivable causation, and they are both an argument with God.

There is mitigation in the Book of Job, of course, since we are shown a purpose behind Job's catastrophe. God starts all the trouble by wagering with the Devil that nothing he can do will shake good Job's faith in Himself. So it is clearly the Evil One who strips Job of his good life in order to destroy his belief in God's justice. And indeed, it turns out that after much twisting and backsliding Job, despite everything, clings to God – and he is promptly rewarded with the return of all his wordly goods plus God's personal gratitude for his having kept the faith. Of course this won't do in our time if only because most of God's argument with Job consists of reminding the poor man of the incomprehensibility of his obscure powers – 'Can you draw out the Leviathan with a fishhook?' and so on. This sort of humiliation is less impressive now when we can press a trigger and destroy whales and might even lift them up with helicopters, and the atom in our hands has the power of a sun. It is the question of justice that we haven't come any closer to clearing up, and indeed the goal of achieving it may be moving further away, so perhaps there is still a little room for *The Man Who Had All The Luck*.

As for the ending of this play – which I am sure I have rewritten twenty times over the past half century, it is as satisfactory as it is possible to be, as complete, let's say, as Job's, which also doesn't quite come down on both feet. The simple fact is that, as moving and imperative as our questioning of our fates may be, there is no possibility of answering the main question – why am I as I am and my life as it is? The more answers one supplies the more new questions arise. David Beeves in this play arrives as close as he can at a workable, conditional faith in the neutrality of the world's intentions toward him. I would emphasize the conditional side of it, but it is better than shooting out your brains in sheer terror of what may happen tomorrow.

The Golden Years, its purplish passages notwithstanding, is a harder if earlier look at passivity and its risks, but here the society as well as an individual is at stake. Montezuma, like the Democracies facing Hitler, was as though hypnotized. Weakened by self-doubt he looks to Cortez, manifestly a brute and a conqueror, as one who may nevertheless bear within him the seed of the future. Something has ended for Montezuma before Cortez ever arrived in Mexico, the heart-lifting glamour of what men call the future is gone out of his life and he can foresee only deadly and meaningless repetition. There was a metaphorical poetry in this in the late Thirties when perfectly intelligent, respectable, even heroic folk like the great flier Charles Lindbergh and his wife Anne could return from a visit to Nazi Germany and called it 'The Wave Of The Future'. I recall feeling myself surrounded in those times by a kind of drifting into cultural suicide and a self-blinded acceptance of murder in high places, and this play was written in alarm. A few years later I did believe that had the Japanese not been deluded enough to attack Pearl Harbor there might well have been sufficient isolationist sentiment in the American people to simply let Hitler have his way with a defeated England and Europe. In a word, our passivity seemed in reality a drift toward an unacknowledged arrangement with Fascism. So – perhaps despite appearances – these are two anti-Fascist plays that were written quite close to the abyss. But perhaps more importantly, they were one very young writer's wrestling with enormous themes.

January 1989, Connecticut, U.S.A.

The Golden Years

A New World Tragedy

What if the glory of escutcheoned doors.
And buildings that a haughtier age designed.
The pacing to and fro on polished floors
Amid great chambers and long galleries,
     lined
With famous portraits of our ancestors!
What if those things the greatest of mankind
Consider most to magnify, or to bless.
But take our greatness with our bitterness?

Rough men-at-arms, cross-gartered to the knees
Or shot in iron, climbed the narrow stairs,
And certain men-at-arms there were
Whose images, in the Great Memory stored,
Come with loud cry and panting breast
To break upon a sleeper's rest
While their great wooden dice beat on the board.

I have loved you better than my soul for all
     my words . . .

William Butler Yeats

THE AZTEC NAMES

Since the Conquistador could not read Aztec symbols, he wrote as he heard. The names are therefore in a nearly phonetic form.

Montezuma	(Just as it spells)
Guatemotzin	(Gwa-te-mótzin)
Cuitlahua	(Cwit-lá-ooah)
Tecuichpo	(Tek-whisch-pó. The 'i*ch*' as in the German 'Rei*ch*')
Xicotenga	(Shi-ko-ténga, the '*sh*' is hard)
The god Quetzalcoatl	(Kwetzal-kwatl)
The god Huitzilpochtli	(Whitzl-pochtli: the '*ch*' again as in 'Rei*ch*')
The commander, Quauhopc	(Kwaw-cowa-páwka)

The Golden Years was given its world premiere on BBC Radio on the 6th November 1987 with the following cast:

MONTEZUMA	Ronald Pickup
GUATEMOTZIN (*His nephew*)	Kim Wall
CUITLAHUA (*His brother*)	John Samson
CAGAMA (*Lord in Council*)	Brian Hewlett
TECUICHPO (*The King's daughter*)	Victoria Carling
PARACH (*The High Priest*)	Hugh Dickson
TALUA (*The history boy*)	Stephen Rashbrook
TAPAIA	Tim Reynolds
QUAUHOPOCA } JUDGE	Norman Jones
AN ASTROLOGER	David Timson
SACRIFICIAL BOY	Stephen Tompkinson
COURIER	Paul Sirr
HERNANDO CORTEZ	John Shrapnel
DONNA MARINA	Hannah Gordon
PEDRO DE ALVARADO	John Hollis
VELASQUEZ DE LEON	Paul Sirr
FRANCISCO DE MONTEJO	Paul Gregory
CRISTOBAL DE OLID	Michael Deacon
DIEGO DE ORDAZ (older)	John Bott
KING XICOTENGA	David Timson
ARBENGA	Steven Harrold
FR. OLMEDO	Norman Bird
MESA	Steven Thompkinson
PANFILO NARVAEZ	John Samson

Directed by Martin Jenkins
Producer's Assistant Julia McLernon
Music by Christos Pittas
Studio managers Sue Templeman, Anne Bunting and Barbara Evans
Announcer John Curle

The publishers acknowledge the help given by the BBC Radio Drama Department in the compilation of the script of **The Golden Years.**

ACT ONE

Scene One

A night in Autumn, 1519.

Tenochtitlan, (now Mexico City), Capital of the Aztec Empire.

This is the Mountain House of Montezuma, King of the Aztec Nation, Emperor of the World. Over the left half of the stage the open sky is seen. A night sky thick with stars. The roof covers only the right half. On a medium level, at its centre is the large throne, built square and low with a high slanting back, and carved with the jagged Aztec design. Up above it two torch lamps burn. In the background the faint outline of mountain peaks at the edge of the sky.

On the rise, the room is lighted only by the torches and the greenish glare of the moon. MONTEZUMA *sits deep in the throne, flanked on a lower level by his council, the Lords* GUATEMOTZIN, *a man of twenty-four and built lithely for war;* CUITLAHUA, *about forty and of slower movement;* CAGAMA, *solid, stocky, about forty-five.* MONTEZUMA, *standing, is watching the* ASTRONOMER *who, charts in hand, is rapidly calculating the stars which he looks up to frequently. On this lowest level, but at the far right,* TAPAIA *stands watching* MONTEZUMA *for the slightest command. Beside the* ASTRONOMER, TALUA, *a boy, stands studying the stars and comparing them with a stone-covered book he holds open in his arms.*

There is no movement, but the astronomer for a moment, the Lords and the King watching him as though waiting for him to say something. MONTEZUMA *glances at the moon, rises slowly, and walks left and stops when he is abreast of the*

ASTRONOMER *but above him.*
All men – deep sonorous chant in background.

MONTEZUMA (*looking up*). My star seems bleeding.
ASTRONOMER (*intent on charts*). The sun is on it, my Lord,
from around the world.
MONTEZUMA (*pause. To* ASTRONOMER). When will you be
finished with your charts and numbers?
ASTRONOMER. A moment more.

MONTEZUMA *looks at the sky. Pause.*

GUATEMOTZIN (*nervously takes a few steps*). The air . . . the
air is growing heavier, Uncle. How much longer before
the moon dies?

ASTRONOMER *lifts hand for silence.* GUATEMOTZIN *feels the
air.*

The air seems to be filling with water.
CUITLAHUA. No wind is a good sign. The flame of the
sacrifice may easily rise to the moon.
GUATEMOTZIN. Is this the way the world ends? Not with
battles, but waiting like old men? Uncle, what are your
thoughts now?
MONTEZUMA. My life and the meaning of it . . . when will
you speak?
ASTRONOMER. The calculations are done, my Lord.

All come toward him anxiously – humming stops.

Look there, the Eastern Star . . .
MONTEZUMA. To the point, how long have we . . . ?
ASTRONOMER. Depending on that star, my Lord. It is
dropping fast, and when it falls behind the horizon, the
speckled moon will ride into eclipse and . . .
CUITLAHUA (*points up*). What's that!
ASTRONOMER. There it is, my Lord, the black tip of the
shadow . . .

MONTEZUMA. I see it now . . .

Distant single drum beat.

ASTRONOMER. It will move across the moon, and if your sacrificial fire does not burn it off, the world is dead this quarter hour.

MONTEZUMA. A quarter hour?

ASTRONOMER. She's black within a quarter, my Lord, no longer.

MONTEZUMA (*slight pause. Nervously*). Perhaps an error . . .?

ASTRONOMER. Impossible. You see, the earth turns on this orbit I have drawn. (*Shows him chart.*) . . . and when the sun revolves . . .

MONTEZUMA. Enough, enough. (*Comes away from him towards centre.*) Tapaia. Bring the sacrifice to me. (*Pause.*) Is my judge dead yet?

TAPAIA. He is being taken to the block now my Lord.

MONTEZUMA. Bring him here . . . hurry. And remember, they must keep an eye on the high road. I am expecting a courier.

TAPAIA *bows . . . starts out.*

CUITLAHUA. Tapaia, wait a moment.

TAPAIA *stops.*

(*To* MONTEZUMA.) My lord, I think it would be wise for you to send a proclamation to the people.

MONTEZUMA. The people? What can I say to the people?

CUITLAHUA. This year was filled with terrors for them, and now the moon, – your word might calm their hearts . . .

MONTEZUMA. Their hearts must not be calmed. They must be terrified tonight, and we, we must be wondrous and searching, not calm. The meanings in this moon we will not read at our ease, but suffering! The sacrifice, Tapaia, hurry.

Exit TAPAIA.

CUITLAHUA (*as* MONTEZUMA *goes up a level*). You are strange tonight, my Lord.

MONTEZUMA. I am all questions, Cuitlahua. (*Looks upward.*)

Drum stops.

CUITLAHUA. And I.

CAGAMA (*anxious, nervous*). When you brothers speak together, I hear. But it's another language, secret between you. Am I dull, my Lord? I am not afraid to die. (*Silence. No answer.*)
When there was a war to fight, I fought. A kingdom to knock down, I was ready with the blow . . . I am not afraid now. I have lived honorably. (*No answer.*) Montezuma, you are wiser, closer to the gods than I. Tell me why I should be afraid. What do you see that I am blind to? The Spaniards, my Lord? If you've proof now that they're gods I'll be happy to join you in welcoming them . . .

CUITLAHUA. Cagama . . .

CAGAMA. No, let me speak if my lord will let me. The time is very short. Montezuma, I am rich and if the Spaniards are proven gods, I'll give them my wealth with all my heart. But I cannot be expected to exult. Not when I know the towns they've wrecked, the countryside they've burned, the black destruction they bring wherever they march. And you've done nothing to stop them, my Lord. I confess, they are nearing the city and my mind is uneasy . . . What do you see in the moon, my Lord? Montezuma, I will not be arrogant! What do you see that I cannot!

MONTEZUMA. I see only what any man might who will open eyes. I tremble under this menacing sky, remembering the hostile shudderings of the earth this year. How the lakes overflowed. Why? . . . without reason; how lightning would strike silently, thunderless; and the stars that fell in the afternoon, – what were the gods striving to tell us? Are we so strong, so proud and tall that when volcanoes fill the air with fiery stones and comets fall like rain we may go our ways indifferent, saying it will be well, we are too great to fall? And now the moon, the moon is shrouding over while striding inward from the East a band of white-faced strangers, unknown to mankind, from out of the sunrise they come calling *my* name. And what am I advised? What wisdom do we draw from such miracles? Pray God for the moon, you say! – we must not die! Slaughter the Spaniards, they've come to conquer! I say the world is agonized, profligate with signs that point to some cancer in the heart of the state: the gods roar warnings in our ears that something must be changed and we're blind and deaf to the signs!

GUATEMOTZIN. But the signs meant the ending of the world.

MONTEZUMA. And more, Guatemotzin – more a thousand-fold than the ending of the world!

Sounds – enter OARACH *and* BOY SACRIFICE.

PARACH. My Lord, our offering to the Gods approaches your Majesty.

MONTEZUMA. May the weight of your step on my threshold bring a blessing to this house.

BOY SACRIFICE. My Lord, my great King!

MONTEZUMA. How beautiful you've grown.

PARACH. He must be on the mountain soon.

MONTEZUMA. I want him here a moment. (*To boy. Smiling.*) You shall hear strange questions in this room. Listen and carry them to heaven in the flame; and I pray you, beg the gods to send us an answer. Roses . . . (*Touches* BOY SACRIFICE.) You're lovely as the flowers you wear . . . (*To Lords*) A god to walk with the gods (*To* BOY SACRIFICE) Are you sad tonight?

BOY SACRIFICE. It has been such a happy year for me, great King.

MONTEZUMA. And you'll not forget how you drank of oldest wine? How you fed on succulent meat? And the concubines we lay at your side on the couch of down, and the perfumed air, you'll not forget?

BOY SACRIFICE. Oh, my Lord, in the flame, in the wind, in the clouds beyond the sun, I will remember this holy year!

PARACH. His pyre is ready, the wood is dry. We stand talking, talking, the moon withers . . .

MONTEZUMA. He will carry a question to the gods.

PARACH. Questions? A priest answers questions. Only a priest . . .

Sound of chains. Enter fettered JUDGE *with* TAPAIA.

JUDGE. Why am I dragged here from the block?

PARACH. Now the Emperor even confers with criminals!

MONTEZUMA. Tapaia bring the courier to me as soon as he arrives.

TAPAIA *disappears.*

Old friend . . .

JUDGE. A judge may claim the privilege of death.

MONTEZUMA. I do not take you from the block to spare you. Nor am I sad that you die a criminal.

JUDGE. I *will* die, Montezuma.

MONTEZUMA. So will all of us perhaps.

JUDGE. But the world will *live* if the flame goes high. And I must not be here when tomorrow comes. I'll kill myself!

MONTEZUMA (*slight pause*). I must know why you're afraid to live. You took a bribe, a rich man, a rich and honoured man – a bribe that would not buy him a sandal for his foot. Why? What calamity is wracking my world that my greatest judge must debase himself?

JUDGE. Let me die . . .

MONTEZUMA. What is your secret? In all our history, no

judge has ever been corrupt. We have no penalty in law for such a crime. How is it possible! Speak!

JUDGE *pauses. He cannot bear to look at the King.*

JUDGE. I have only horrors to tell you, my Lord, let me go!

MONTEZUMA. I have seen horrors this year. I can bear another!

JUDGE. My Lord, you fought your last war a year ago. When that war finished, I looked out on the world. There is hardly a rise of ground left for you to conquer, Montezuma.

MONTEZUMA. Aye, all horizons are garrisoned.

JUDGE. Then where is the further glory? What step can you take but downward?

GUATEMOTZIN. The man is mad, my Lord! Take him away!

MONTEZUMA. No. Let him speak!

JUDGE. Then I saw the waters rising. I saw the silent lightning, and the comets falling. I could not sleep, what did they mean? I walked the streets of your cities, listened to the people, the potter, the jeweller, the monger, and the fisherman. 'The price is high', they said, 'I am a poor man'. 'Crops are good', they say, 'but I starve for food.' 'I had a son, they took him for the wars.' Whispering, the cities of empire sullen, whispering: 'Montezuma? He lives like a god and we suffer.' 'How long? How long? How long? How long?'

GUATEMOTZIN. Stop it!

JUDGE. Would the gods I could! But between the lips of both oceans the empire is cracking!

The Lords are furious.

GUATEMOTZIN. Insolent man!

MONTEZUMA. Leave him! (*Quiet.*) He sees it too.

CAGAMA (*astounded*). Sees what my lord?

MONTEZUMA. The empire is cracking, Cagama. (*Pause.*)

The gods are loitering here, let the truth confront them.
(*To the* JUDGE.) And you thought, how the situation
might be saved?

JUDGE. I did, until that dawn three months ago, when the
Spaniards landed on the Eastern coast.

MONTEZUMA. (*To boy*). Hear it, Holy Boy, hear it now!
(*To* JUDGE.) And what did you think then?

JUDGE. You wove the tapestry of Mexico but now the
threads run out.

GUATEMOTZIN. How can you listen to him Uncle?

MONTEZUMA (*rapidly*). You've seen it from below; what
will mend the cracking? How would you mend the state
if you were king?

GUATEMOTZIN. Troops made it and troops will mend it!
The whip will shut their mouths!

MONTEZUMA. Aye, and for how long, how long, Guatemotzin?

GUATEMOTZIN. Until they whisper again, then whip
again!

MONTEZUMA. And if it only cracks wider still?

Pause.

JUDGE. Now you are wise! You have reached the hour where
force no more will rule the state . . .

MONTEZUMA. Yes . . .

JUDGE. And force will not bind up its rotting limbs.

MONTEZUMA. Hear it. (*To boy*.) Holy Boy, hear it, a
question for the gods! – This is the horror I see rising on
the state, the question that the writhing universe has
thrown up in my brain; – how shall I rule if not with the
sword!

JUDGE. Die with me now, Montezuma!

MONTEZUMA. Die!

JUDGE. Now, at the zenith of your glory, die as you lived;
Emperor of the World, or you'll crumble furious in
storms.

CAGAMA. He dare not . . . !

GUATEMOTZIN AND LORDS. Kill him! Kill the madman!

JUDGE. (*To Lords*). You are the madmen! Fools! Mad with power and the riches you hold! Your day is over. The people are reaching for arms! Him they'll follow, but where? Can he lead them to conquer the oceans? If you love this King let him die in glory!

MONTEZUMA. Enough!

JUDGE. My Lord . . . !

MONTEZUMA. I would die with you now for I see the same horror. But I'll not believe that all I've built, my golden cities, my roads, my gardens, aqueducts and spires, my state, my Aztec state unparalleled on earth before – I'll not believe they rose out of the earth for spiders to devour.

JUDGE. Everything dies!

MONTEZUMA. Not this! This will end only with the world! There must be a way to govern that does not end in ruins!

JUDGE. But if you can't rule by force can you rule without it? Therefore the thing is finished!

CAGAMA. I don't understand! My lord, are we all mad? How can you govern except by force?

ASTRONOMER. My lord, the shadow is moving quickly!

All look up at the moon.

MONTEZUMA (*still looking up. It is quiet*). Parach, will the sacrificial flame soar so high?

PARACH. Emperor, what is turning in your mind? How can you rule without force?

MONTEZUMA. Parach, will the world go on?

PARACH. I pray for a tall flame.

MONTEZUMA. Then I bid you, Holy Boy, tell this to the gods in heaven. I, Montezuma, made this nation in the way I knew – and war was enough for a king to know. But what the sword has won the sword alone cannot keep safe. But I am not sad; I know that my thoughts come to me from heaven, although I do not always understand them. But

I have imagined rivers of flowing brass where swords and shields have melted, and I often think of times before our fathers, and their fathers before them – when the world was young and a man-god lived on this ground we love, and he ruled here with a soft voice and never touched weapons. You know his name, Holy Boy, our Quetzalcuatl god, gentle Lord of the moving wind, the white god who walked into the sunrise and with his going, murder burst on the world, and war. But he promised to return one day . . .

GUATEMOTZIN. These Spaniards are murdering . . . !

MONTEZUMA. 'I will return!' he said, 'and the Golden Years will shine again from my outstretched hands.'

GUATEMOTZIN. How could *they* be . . . ?

MONTEZUMA (*to* BOY SACRIFICE). The Spaniards are white, and they came from the sunrise! It's true they've come calling commands, ruthless; but I've not stopped them and I will not raise a hand until I know; are they God's children, or mortal strangers coming for conquest? Go now; beg the spirits, send this King a sign to go by; in the trees, in the sky, brand them with a name! Are they men or gods? They're close now. If I must kill again, it must be soon. Take him Parach, take him to the mountain top. And may the flame of your strong body burn us onward to a stronger year! Farewell, Holy Boy.

BOY SACRIFICE. I will ask the spirits to send my Lords a sign; farewell.

ASTRONOMER. The time is short, my Lord!

MONTEZUMA. Hurry, Parach, and let the flame climb heavenward from his burning heart!

PARACH *and the boy go out. There is a pause.*

CAGAMA. I understand nothing . . .

GUATEMOTZIN. My Lord . . . is war . . . my life and all I've learned and worshipped . . . suddenly to be despised?

MONTEZUMA. Try to understand . . . and you, Cagama . . . (*Breaks off angrily.*) I am not mad; a better time has never been for gods to return . . . Brother, my Lords, does not one prince tremble with me! The gods may have returned!

CUITLAHUA. I am ready to believe.

MONTEZUMA (*eagerly*). You have received a sign Cuitlahua?

CAGAMA. My lord, I see only *your* eyes. All my cities and I will travel by the clear conviction of those stars.

MONTEZUMA. That is good. And you, Guatemotzin, your cities?

GUATEMOTZIN. If there is a sign . . . then I'll bow to Spaniards. But how a peaceful god can sack your towns . . .

CUITLAHUA. But the people resist, they must be put aside . . .

GUATEMOTZIN. Put aside, and raped! Uncle, I know I am too young to understand, but if they're men, we're opening the gates to conquerors, and . . .

MONTEZUMA. *Four hundred* conquerors. I can muster eighty thousand troops this hour. Be sure of it, Guatemotzin, if they're men they'll die as all my enemies have died!

Enter TAPAIA, *hurrying.*

TAPAIA. The courier is in sight, my Lord, coming down the high road from the East.

ASTRONOMER. The moon is almost covered! The stars are fading!

MONTEZUMA. Hurry, bring him to me!

Exit TAPAIA. *A man laughs quietly.*

(*Startled.*) Ah!

Man laughs again.

I had forgotten you.

JUDGE. But death forgets no one, my Lord.

MONTEZUMA. Spare me your wisdom. Go – take him! – Go, and be a good example for the country; die bravely, as befits one of Montezuma's judges.

JUDGE. I will die with my memories of Aztec hands building a world. The stones now are dropping from the walls . . . I see dust rising . . .

Enter TECUICHPO.

TECUICHPO. Don't let him say any more Father!

MONTEZUMA. Tecuichpo.

TECUICHPO. Take him away!

JUDGE. I pray the Montezuma king will not outlive his honour.

MONTEZUMA. Take him.

Exit JUDGE.

TECUICHPO. There is some spirit here; making us mad Father . . . I must not keep it from you – I have prayed in the Temple . . . it came upon me suddenly to pray . . . that they will come here to us.

GUATEMOTZIN. You prayed in the Temple for Spaniards?

TECUICHPO. It was like a great hand on my back, pressing me upward . . .

GUATEMOTZIN. She has prayed for your death, Uncle!

TECUICHPO. No. Not death, Guatemotzin! . . . for the coming-to-life of my dreams!

MONTEZUMA. You dreamed . . . ?

GUATEMOTZIN. They've poisoned the air we breathe!

MONTEZUMA. Tell me what you dreamed!

TECUICHPO. A thousand dreams, father, since the hour they touched the coast they have walked into my nights; brightly, brightly father, like the sun on wet rock, and I must see them now, how they move, and how they talk

. . . I want to touch their eyes . . . !

GUATEMOTZIN. And if it's conquerors you've prayed for!

MONTEZUMA. What did they say, did they speak?

TECUICHPO. Like rivers, with the voices of rivers . . . last night they gave me a white swan . . . (*Recalling.*) and it died in my hands . . . I had –

MONTEZUMA. A swan died . . . ?

TECUICHPO (*seeing their fright*). What does that mean? Oh, Father, I can't have prayed for conquerors! Guatemotzin, there *will* be a wedding in the Spring! (*Sees they draw from her.*) Why do you turn from me? Then attack with your armies; I don't want them here – who will forgive my wicked heart!

A slight pause. MONTEZUMA *turns to* CUITLAHUA, *wonderingly.*

MONTEZUMA. I have never known such a dream . . . a white swan, and it died . . .

Sudden booming of drums in distance.

ASTRONOMER. The stars are gone!

GUATEMOTZIN. The drums!

TAPAIA. Here is the courier from the coast, my Lord.

As they all start towards the open sky, enter TAPAIA *supporting* COURIER. MONTEZUMA *rushes to him.*

MONTEZUMA. Speak. Have you seen the Spaniards!

COURIER. A great battle is preparing, my Lord. In Tlascalla, fifty thousand troops are facing the Spaniards!

CAGAMA (*joyously*). *Fifty thousand!* Tlascalla is standing up to them!

MONTEZUMA. You left before the battle started?

GUATEMOTZIN. Tlascalla will wipe them out!

MONTEZUMA (*to* COURIER). But you saw no fighting?

COURIER. No, my Lord. But I thought you should see this

before the moon goes dark . . . I stole it from their camp as you commanded . . .

He hands MONTEZUMA *a cloth-covered object.*

MONTEZUMA. This . . . this is . . .

MONTEZUMA *uncovers it in silence but for the rising drumbeats in the distance. All eyes glued to it . . . as the cloth falls from it, the drums suddenly get louder and . . .*

COURIER. His helmet, my Lord. Cortez wore it on his head.

ASTRONOMER. Montezuma . . . the moon is black!

MONTEZUMA. Tapaia, the torch! (*Still eyeing the helmet.*) Now we'll know what they are . . .

CAGAMA. What does it mean . . . ?

TECUICHPO. Look at all the people on the mountain!

MONTEZUMA. On the head of the Quetzalcoatl god who stands in the Temple is the metal helmet he left behind, when he departed into the sun . . .

CUITLAHUA. Compare them!

ASTRONOMER. A falling star! Signal the mountain, Montezuma! Burn the Holy Boy!

MONTEZUMA. My Lords . . . if the moon returns and lights up the world again we'll go to the Temple, compare this with the headpiece of the god, and if they match! – The gods have come; we . . .

TECUICHPO. Oh, Father, I'm afraid now!

GUATEMOTZIN. And if they do not match!

ASTRONOMER (*frenzied*). They're waiting for the signal! My lord, the torch . . .

MONTEZUMA. Signal the mountain to start the sacrifice!

An Aztec horn is blown which echoes through the atmosphere.

GUATEMOTZIN. My Lord, if they are not at all the same!

TECUICHPO. The sky is lower!

CUITLAHUA. They're lighting the pyre!

MONTEZUMA. Pray God to return us the world; we attack

tomorrow if they're not the same. And the waiting's done, and we'll drive the Spaniard back to the sea!

The sky reflects a rising fire.

CUITLAHUA. The flame! Look, the mountain is burning!

GUATEMOTZIN. The smoke leaps to heaven!

The drumming becomes louder.

CUITLAHUA. It's reaching for the shadow! Like morning!

TECUICHPO. The sky is closer! The world is burning!

CUITLAHUA. The flame is red! The boy is burning now, my Lord!

GUATEMOTZIN. Look at the mountain, bright as the sunrise!

Pause.

CAGAMA. Why doesn't it move?

TECUICHPO. The shadow's not moving from the moon . . . oh, my wicked heart!

ASTRONOMER. The world is standing still! It is the end!

The wind rises suddenly during the invocation. There is humming behind his invocation.

MONTEZUMA (*calls up to the heavens*).
  I call to the lightning!
  Strike out of slumber!
  Crack open the tomb!
  I call to the stars;
  Light on the world again!
  Thunder in the clouds again!
  On mountains we burn, burning the beautiful,
  I call to all gods, and the god of all;
  Return us the light,
  Resurrect the shrouded moon! . . .

ASTRONOMER (*hushed*). My Lord . . . the wind!

MONTEZUMA (*feeling it*). Wind?

CUITLAHUA (*alarmed*). . . . Suddenly . . .

GUATEMOTZIN (*opening his palm to it*). . . . Feel it . . . how swift . . .

ASTRONOMER (*fearful*). My Lord, the moon is not moving . . .

Pause.

CAGAMA (*the fright grows*). It's flattening out . . .

GUATEMOTZIN. The people are running away!

CUITLAHUA. Brother, the flame's blowing out!

MONTEZUMA. No!

ASTRONOMER. My Lord, the end!!

MONTEZUMA (*rushes out to the sky, throws his arms out, and roars . . .*). Stop the wind! STOP THE WIND!

CUITLAHUA. It's out! The fire is out!!

They stand fixed, staring at the black sky, MONTEZUMA's hands rigid over his head. A long silence when the faintest greenish light sprays the sky and their faces. MONTEZUMA's arms come down slowly to his sides. The others survey the sky, mystified.

(*Softly, struck.*) The flame did not rise.

CAGAMA. How can it be . . . ?

TECUICHPO. The stars . . . !

GUATEMOTZIN (*facing the moon*). The moon is shining again . . . why . . . how . . . ?

GUATEMOTZIN turns to MONTEZUMA with the others. MONTEZUMA turns slowly from the moon to the helmet which gleams brightly in the moonlight. They follow his eyes. He goes softly, lifts it as though it were alive. All are entranced by it. He turns it over in his hands again, then raises his eyes to them. They return the look wide-eyed and transfixed with fearful wonder as the light fades into complete darkness.

Scene Two

All men required.

The gloomy interior of a deserted temple several days march from the capital. Night. As the light goes up MESA, *a young fellow, not armoured, approaches clutching his arm . . . followed by* FR. OLMEDO *supporting* ORDAZ, *a giant man who is gulping down air . . .*

MESA. It's broke, my arm – it's broken! (*Looks around.*) Where are we? What is this place?

FR. OLMEDO. Lie down here, Ordaz . . .

ORDAZ (*almost weeping, flaying his arms about . . .*). The horses! The devil damned horses did it!

FR. OLMEDO. There will be other battles, Diego. Mary watches over us . . .

MESA (*clutching his arm*). My arm, Padre!

As FR. OLMEDO *goes to him, enter* CAPTAINS *and a few* SOLIDERS *limping, holding an arm, etc. . . . and one frantically searching himself as though he'd lost something. All talk breathlessly and vociferously at once, followed a moment later by* CORTEZ *and* MARINA *who is patting his neck with a cloth. As their words become distinguishable and they enter the lighted area . . .*

LEON (*to* MONTEJO). Where in hell were the cannon, Montejo?

MONTEJO. Where they should've been! – I couldn't fire into Spaniards, could I? . . .

OLID. You should've shot them off in the air! . . .

MARINA nurses CORTEZ who sits.

ARBENGA. They were all loaded . . .!

OLID (*to* ARBENGA). Shut your mouth, Arbenga!

MESA (*to* OLID). There was no time for cannon . . . !

LEON (*to* MESA). Damned Italian blunderer!

MESA. Damn yourself . . .

ORDAZ (*from the floor. To* LEON). Don't curse the cannoniers, you puppy!

LEON (*turns on him*). I spit on cannoniers!

ORDAZ. And I spit on your stinkin' horses!

LEON. The horses saved our lives!

ORDAZ. The foot-solider saved your lives! Montejo, what did the horses do but box us in so we couldn't fire a cannon without hitting our own people?

LEON. You can't gallop a horse on those rocks!

ORDAZ. Then why in Lucifer's hell didn't you get out of the way!?

OLID. That's easy to say!

ORDAZ. Ship your cows back to Cuba, for Jesus sake; every time I lift a sword there's a horse's ass in my face!

CORTEZ. Señores! (*Quiet.*) There is still work to be done. Leon, be so good as to see that the horses are watered.

LEON. Hernando, you're bleeding . . .

CORTEZ. A flesh wound in the neck. And I couldn't find my helmet. Go, Leon. Montejo . . .

LEON. I'll find some water for you . . .

CORTEZ. Do as I say. See to the horses.

LEON. Aye . . . take care of him, Marina.

Exit LEON.

CORTEZ. Montejo, see your cannon are kept loaded . . .

MONTEJO. It was impossible to fire, Hernando . . .

CORTEZ. I know, I know. Go on . . . what are you searching for?

MONTEJO. My purse . . . it's been stolen by the infidel.

CORTEZ (*wry smile*). Maybe that's why the cannon didn't go off.

The men laugh.

MONTEJO. You mustn't say that, Hernando . . .

CORTEZ (*suddenly angering but restraining himself*). I am saying, Montejo! – The cannon fell asleep like drunkards clutching a purse!

MONTEJO. I am ready to weep, Hernando . . .

CORTEZ. Be ready to fight, Señor, and we'll live longer! Now see to your cannon.

Pause. MONTEJO *goes out, ashamed.*

CORTEZ. Pedro, will you . . . ? (*Looks around near him.*) Pedro . . . where is Alvarado! (*Stands quickly.*)

OLID. He must be with the men . . .

CORTEZ. Is he hurt, did you see him?

OLID. No, but . . .

CORTEZ. Find him, Olid . . . go and find Alvarado . . . Pedro . . . go with him . . . find Pedro . . .

FR. OLMEDO. I'm sure he's safe . . .

CORTEZ. How you all love to *talk*! Go and find Alvarado!!

FR. OLMEDO *hurries out,* OLID *more leisurely . . . after a few steps, he turns.*

OLID (*softly*). It was a blunder, Hernando.

CORTEZ. Señor de Olid, I appreciate your learning, but will you spare me strategy and find Alvarado?

OLID (*bows with a touch of sarcasm*). I spare you strategy.

He goes out.

CORTEZ (*calling after* OLID). And see to the wounded! Ordaz, can you walk?

ORDAZ. I'm tired, Hernando.

CORTEZ. Follow him? He'll stir up trouble again I think.

ORDAZ (*rises with difficulty*). Ahh . . . (*He's almost weeping.*) I hate that man. Despise him!

CORTEZ. But will you go and follow him?

ORDAZ. You're different, Hernando. You're a horseman but a foot-soldier is not dirt to you. I tell you the foot-solider is the heart of this army!

CORTEZ. I know, Diego, follow him.

ORDAZ (*starts and stops*). What will be the end of it, Hernando. We can't fight another such battle.

CORTEZ. God is with us, Captain.

ORDAZ. Aye . . . Find a way, Hernando, I'm an old man, but I'm not meant to die here. We'll not die here, Hernando!

CORTEZ. We'll live to be Kings, Diego.

ORDAZ (*smiles sadly*). How sweet you are . . . Christ will speak to you . . . (*Rushes to him weeping, kisses his cheek, embraces him.*) Think, Hernando, think . . . we must not die here! (*To* MESA.) Come with me, Mesa.

MESA. My arm . . .

ORDAZ. Let him think . . . come on. (MESA *does not move.*) Italian!

MESA. I'm coming.

ORDAZ (*assuringly*). Don't worry for Alvarado . . . and think, Hernando, there must be a way out of this . . . I'll follow Señor de Olid the intellectual . . .

Some mocking laughter.

ORDAZ *hurries out with* MESA *behind him.* MARINA *is alone with* CORTEZ, *standing behind him patting his neck with the cloth. He is seated. He stretches out his right leg and squeezes the muscle of his thigh, staring straight ahead. She comes around, kneels before him and massages his thigh, he tightens with the pain. She stops then continues more softly.*

CORTEZ. What is this building?

MARINA. A temple. They deserted it when we came.

CORTEZ (*looks about*). You're weeping, Marina.

MARINA. No.

CORTEZ. Why?

MARINA (*slight pause*). I thought you would die. They aimed for you . . . all of them . . . for your face!

CORTEZ. They know me now. (*Pause.*) You're not weeping for me, Marina.

MARINA. Who then?

CORTEZ. The enemy.

MARINA. The enemy are people too.

CORTEZ (*looks at her, lifts her chin*). Your eyes are so dark now. You used to smile always.

MARINA (*she gets up*). Tell me, Hernando, how long must you go on killing?

CORTEZ. Sometimes men must kill to bring a blessing.

MARINA. Never, Hernando, never.

CORTEZ. You're so foolish . . . this is war . . .

MARINA. But I didn't come with you to fight wars . . .

CORTEZ. How else can we make them Christians?

MARINA. As you told me Christ made Christians.

CORTEZ (*smiles*). Yes, but, these people are not . . .

MARINA. They are not animals! They are not to be burned as you've burned them, stabbed as you've stabbed them . . . Hernando, ten thousand childen are fatherless since you marched from the coast!

CORTEZ. Stop it!

MARINA. Turn back!

CORTEZ. Eh? Marina, what did you say? (*He rises.*)

MARINA. Turn back to the coast. I'll lead you as I led you here . . .

CORTEZ. I don't want you to utter those words again, Marina.

MARINA. You can't . . .

CORTEZ (*flares up*). Never again!! Never. (*She lowers her eyes. He strides from her, turns to her . . . almost appealing.*) What can I do? Would you have me go out to them without arms, without . . .

MARINA. Without arms, without blood . . . I would walk with a cross before you. I would speak to them, 'People, good people, hear the voice of the True God!' They would listen . . .

CORTEZ. How pure you are . . . They would never listen. They would wipe us out . . .

MARINA. Then we would die, and God would remember us. Hernando, I walked alone out of the forest to meet you. I was the first, – why? – to kill? I had enough of killing; my father died in battle, I was sold to another who died in war, captured again in war . . . over the face of Mexico I ran before the storm, – peace was the star I sought, and peace was the word you gave me. Peace on earth, you said, and I believed it. The white sails of your ships, full in the wind, – I knew at the sight of them heaving on the waves – this was clean, and I walked on the beach to touch you, to believe in you, and now. I'm killing with you . . . killing my people.

CORTEZ. When you stood that day on the sunlit deck, the holy water still wet on your cheeks, what did I say to you? Marina, we will tear this people from the claws of anti-christ and Jesus will reign in Mexico and blood and stone will not stop us!

MARINA. But what has killing brought you? Here you are; Hernando – you have less than four hundred men now and out there fifty thousand people are gathering to fight again! What force will save you now!

CORTEZ (*desperately*). My sword and Christ will save us now!

MARINA. Go back, Hernando . . . !

CORTEZ. Enough!!

He raises his hand as though to strike her. She springs away as though he'd done it before. We hear ALVARADO *call* 'HERNANDO' *off stage. Enter* ALVARADO *hurrying, leading a struggling indian girl by a rope tied around her waist* . . .

(*With deep joy.*) Pedro! Are you hurt!

ALVARADO. Only my heart! Hernando . . . look. (*Indicates the girl.*) Every time we capture women what happens to

mine? I go to sleep and by morning, psst! . . . Some
bastard's son is riding her under my nose. So this time I
resolved, – Alvarado, find thee a rope. Result? I'll tie this
one to my leg and sleep in peace.

Laughter.
*Sound of grumbling men coming closer and entering. All turn
towards doorway except* MARINA *who crosses to girl and
talks to her quietly.*

(*Confidentially.*) Hernando . . . there's going to be
trouble.

CORTEZ. What trouble?

ALVARADO. The men say the Tlascallans are bringing up
more troops . . .

CORTEZ. Who told them that?

ALVARADO. Some of them want to retreat . . .

CORTEZ. Who's spreading this?

ALVARADO. I think it's Cristobal de Olid.

CORTEZ. Ah? And what do they want me to do?

ALVARADO. I don't know, but speak to them, they only
need your word . . .

MARINA *comes quickly from girl.*

MARINA. Alvarado . . . this girl is twelve-years-old.

ALVARADO. I know, but she seems . . .

MARINA. Hernando, she's a child!

CORTEZ (*hearing men entering*). Shut up . . . !

Enter Captains ORDAZ, MONTEJO, LEON *and* FR.
OLMEDO. *These come forward silently and flank* CORTEZ,
turning to watch the SOLDIERS *come in.*

Come in, good soliders! Let the wounded sit! Well now
. . . what can I do for you, dear friends?

The SOLDIERS *enter the lighted area, sullen, those behind
growling, etc. They halt. The officers flanking* CORTEZ *are*

*facing the men, whose ranks seem to reach far back into the
shadows. All of those visible are bandaged on some part of
their bodies.*

CORTEZ (*he inspects each face, identifying them. He turns and
looks over his officers. To the men.*) Speak. What is it?
(*Silence. To his officers.*) One of my officers then? (*They
don't speak. To the men.*) Señores, I am ashamed of you.
What brings you here?

ARBENGA (*steps forward, doffs his cap*). Señor Cortez,
we . . .

CORTEZ. Arbenga.

ARBENGA. Yes, Captain, I'm no trouble-maker. But . . .
we've fought . . . like Spaniards. And, what have we got
for it?

CORTEZ. Before the mason finishes the house he cannot
sleep in it.

ARBENGA (*looks at him blankly*). Yes. (*Nods. Turns to men.*)
Alfredo . . . (ALFREDO *tries to edge back into the crowd.*
ARBENGA *grabs his wrist and drags him forward.*) Tell him
what you told me!

ALFREDO (*frightened, dumb*). I only . . .

ARBENGA (*yells*). Tell him!! Won't one of you tell him?

ARBENGA *turns to all of them appealingly to say something,
but they're cold. He turns quickly to Captain de Olid.*

Captain Olid.

OLID *draws away from him.*

CORTEZ. Ah?! (*To* OLID.) Can *you* explain, Cristobal de
Olid?

OLID. I? Why do you ask me? I have nothing to do with this!

CORTEZ. Come, Cristobal, speak up for this rebellion!

OLID. Arbenga! – Have I spoken to you of rebellion?

ARBENGA (*looks at* OLID, *pause*). No, Captain de Olid. (*To*
CORTEZ.) Señor, I am a simple man. I know only what

I see. I came from Cuba for gold. I was prepared to fight for it. And we fought, – aye, señor, – how did we fight, ten thousand upon thousand of heathen and we slew them all. And some of us died, and tonight not one of us is without a wound.

CORTEZ. Aye; when there is war there are wounds, you speak truly.

ARBENGA (*points outside*). If you will look, señor, more than fifty thousand Tlascallans are gathering out there on the plain below.

CORTEZ (*simply*). I have seen them.

ARBENGA. Aye, and there are three hundred and eighty-five Spaniards alive tonight?

Silence.

We can't hold them off again. I beg you, Captain, let us not die among the heathen: lead us go back to the coast.

CORTEZ. And then, what?

ARBENGA (*hesitates*). We wish to return to Cuba.

CORTEZ. Cuba? (*Angering.*) I never heard of gold in Cuba.

VOICE 1 (*from among the men far back*). But who's rich from the gold in Mexico!

VOICES. Aye!

CORTEZ (*straining over the heads of the men. Pointing*) *You* will be rich! (*Some laughter.*) Hey? Do you think you stand in a barren forest here? This is the gateway to an empire and we've got our toe in the crack! (*Walks up a level.*) Climb the trees and look to the Western hills where Montezuma sits! Gold you say? – The very sky glares yellow over that golden city! Spit on Cuba, spit on it, I say!

Dead silence. No response.

ALVARADO (*yelling at them*). You frogs! (*Dashes up and down before them.*) You bloody whoreson cowards!

CORTEZ. Pedro!!

ALVARADO (*waving his sword*). By God's blood I swear
 I'll . . . !

CORTEZ. Put away your sword, Alvarado!

> ALVARADO *subsides, turns, spits towards* OLID, *and walks
> glaring at him.*

CORTEZ (*to men*). Think. Where are you running? Cuba? –
 The lazy air and the day sleeping on your shoulders; the
 bloodless women smiling for your purse . . . is this for
 Spaniards? And did you forget the fleet? Remember,
 Señores, we scuttled the fleet in Vera Cruz harbour when
 we came. Every ship but one lies at the bottom. Have you
 forgotten how we stood on the shore and cried, 'sink the
 fleet, we'll fight this land until we're kings in it!' *There*
 were Spaniards!

VOICE 2 (*holds up his bandaged arms and rushes forward*). I'm
 wounds and scabs from head to foot! I can't lift a sword.

SOLDIERS (*roar*). He's right! Back to Cuba! Back to Cuba.

CORTEZ (*roaring back*). Do I not bleed!! In the neck? Here
 . . . in both legs!? (*Silence.*) What did you expect if not
 bleeding? Did you come to play with flowers? Did I tell
 you Montezuma would hand you his head on a dish, or
 did I say we'd kill for it! What did I tell you and what
 did you come for! Answer me that!!

> *Pause.*

OLID. May I answer that, Hernando?

> CORTEZ *doesn't turn around for a moment. Then slowly he
> turns and moves toward him.*

CORTEZ. You have something to say now, Captain de Olid?

OLID. Aye, Captain Cortez, I have something to say.

> *The captains move toward him threateningly. He quickly
> starts to speak.*

Señores. Captain Cortez forgets one very important fact.

We shipped on this expedition not to conquer Mexico at
all.

SOLDIERS. He's right . . . he's telling truth!

OLID. On the contrary, we had explicit orders from Señor
Velasquez, Governor of Cuba, to scour the coast for trade
and were forbidden to march inland!

CAPTAINS. Stop it . . . that's enough! (*Etc.* . . .)

SOLDIERS. Let him speak! Go on!

OLID. But what happened! Certain officers among us
became – how shall I say – ambitious. And the night
before we sailed, decided in secret, mind you, that we
were going on this suicidal expedition to conquer Mexico!
(*Shouts for and against.*) Finally! Finally, I say! When the
plot leaked out to the Governor's ear, CORTEZ pulled
anchor and sailed that night before the Governor could
stop him! In short, those of you who love your country
will decide to return to it because we sailed on a stolen
fleet; under the law, we are bandits and are therefore
cursed by God!

The SOLDIERS' *shouts of approval are loudest.* CORTEZ
*draws his sword, leaps to the platform and jabs it down into
the crowd. Sudden silence.*

CORTEZ. What are you – peasants! I picked no farmers for
the fleet! I took hidalgos, Spaniards, conquistadors,
fighters with blood to give!!

VOICE 2. Back to Cuba!

MEN. Cuba! Cuba! (*Etc.*)

CORTEZ. All right, you pigs, you stupid oxen, you bungling
bottom-lice! Back to Cuba, come on!

The men cheer.

(*Mocking them.*) Aye! Hurrah! Hurrah! (*Quiet.*) But of
course, brave Señores, valiant conquistadors, the
moment we set foot on Cuban soil we'll hang for high
treason! (*Silence.*) What . . . no cheers? Why not? Cuba?

Come on, to Cuba! You think the flags will fly when you reach Santiago! Governor Velasquez will crush you like rats! To him you're thieves, mockers of his authority, stinking scum of the earth!

SOLDIER (*from deep back*). Make way! Make way!

The crowd opens up and a Spanish soldier comes rushing through.

CORTEZ. Well?

SOLDIER. Captain, their King wants an audience with you at once.

CORTEZ. What! (*Comes down quickly.*)

SOLDIER. King Xicotenga, the King of this country, he's waiting beyond the lines.

CORTEZ. Marina, what would this mean?

MARINA. This is how they bring an ultimatum.

CORTEZ. Go and tell him to come here. And keep a clear eye on their troops.

SOLDIER. Aye, Captain.

CORTEZ. Hurry!

SOLDIER *exits.*

(CORTEZ *jumps up to the level.*) To your positions now. If we must fight, fight we will and like Christians and Spaniards. Do I hear your answer?

Men pause. They start to turn, obeying, but sullenly.

Wait, señores!

They stop.

I promise you I will try to avoid a battle. But it may be we will have to fight . . . Do you hear? Señores!

Silence.

Then remember this, we have come so far and vanquished forty thousand at a time not because of

strength or swordplay. Divinity, Señores, the unconquer-
able Spanish name, the gods in our speech, in our
prancing horse, in the wild glare of our armour – these
are what we've ridden on, and conquered on. But let
them once see us turn our backs, and we will fight as
armoured *men*, not gods but *men*, and we are done!
(*Pause.*) So, we are Christians and conquistadors, from
this night on we fling across these purple hills a voice of
terror as a *god* would fling – aye, gods in iron with thunder
beating out – attack if we must, and to victory! To your
posts, Señores. Those who are not badly injured remain
here. Adios!

The men go out.

Leon, go outside and mount your horse. Wait until the
King comes in – then, give her the whip and gallop right
past this doorway. Do it every few minutes and plenty of
noise mind. You understand?

LEON (*smiles*). Aye.

CORTEZ (*as* LEON *goes*). At full gallop!

LEON (*smiles again*). She'll sound like thunder.

Exit LEON *at a lope.*

CORTEZ (*to the* CAPTAINS *and remaining men*). Remember
we are a victorious army treating indignantly for peace.
We are deeply offended that they dared attack us. The
face is determined, the bearing, proud, – erect, Montejo.
This time, when I touch my breastplate, so, (*he does so*)
everyone cries out in anger.

ALVARADO. *And* half-draw our swords.

CORTEZ. That's good. And half-draw the sword. (*To*
SOLDIER 2.) You bring me the King . . . alone!

SOLDIER 2. Yes, sir.

Exit SOLDIER.

ALVARADO. I think our bandages should come off,

Hernando.

CORTEZ. Yes, yes. Off with them. Quickly.

MESA. My arm'll bleed.

CORTEZ. Take it off, Mesa!

As they take off their visible bandages.

Erect now! (*He inspects them.*) Gonzalo, no stick.

GONZALO. My knee . . .

CORTEZ. Gonzalo! (*Kicks the stick from under him and shoves it aside as the* SOLDIER *enters.*) No stick.

The men chuckle.

SOLDIER 2. The King, Señor.

CORTEZ (*looks at all the men*). Marina, stay here beside me. Alvarado, here on my left (*A final inspection.*) Now bring him in.

Enter King XICOTENGA. *He is in his prime, tall, proud, lithe. He comes part way in. Runs his eyes along the soliders. Comes further in, warily, but unafraid, inspects the Captains, his eyes stop at* CORTEZ.

XICOTENGA. You are Hernando Cortez?

CORTEZ. And you, Your Majesty, the renowned Xicotenga. I regret the state of my accommodation for you.

XICOTENGA. It was more comfortable before we stripped it bare.

CORTEZ. An unnecessary precaution, your Majesty, we will not be with you long.

XICOTENGA. I have come to tell you that. You will depart my territory this hour.

CORTEZ (*pause, smiles.*) Surely you are not serious, my lord.

XICOTENGA (*motions outside*). I have sixty thousand troops in the valley.

CORTEZ. And I have a hundred thousand outside that doorway.

XICOTENGA. A pity they refused to fight with you today.

CORTEZ. Oh, they did not refuse, señor, I simply dislike slaughter. But perhaps you would like to meet . . . say a thousand of them.

XICOTENGA (*smiling*). I would be honoured.

Fierce gallop of hooves past the doorway. XICOTENGA *starts, then quickly composes himself. During the noise* CORTEZ *shouts something to* ALVARADO. *As it dies down,* ALVARADO *stands looking incredulously at* CORTEZ.

CORTEZ. Go, Captain, bring in the soliders.

ALVARADO *goes out.*

(*Comes very close to the King, talks into his face, but still smiling*). You realize of course, that your people are still alive because I preferred not to kill them yet.

XICOTENGA. I . . .

CORTEZ. But you must realize that!

XICOTENGA. I will wipe you out in an hour.

CORTEZ. You truly believe that . . . ? (*He looks straight into his eyes for a moment, then smiles.*) Are you aware that I am in your country only because it lies on the road to Montezuma?

XICOTENGA. What do you want with the Aztec?

CORTEZ. I want to conquer him.

XICOTENGA (*amused*). *You* will conquer Montezuma?

CORTEZ. I never lie, Señor.

XICOTENGA. You are his enemy and he lets you come so far? He would crush you with the rise of his smallest finger!

CORTEZ. In a word, Señor, Montezuma is afraid of Spaniards. He dares not attack us!

XICOTENGA (*he slowly looks about at the officers and men, then back to* CORTEZ). In one hour, I attack. My people despise you. They'll not rest until every one of you is dead. One hour, Cortez; farewell.

He turns. As he starts to walk the hooves gallop past the doorway violently. He stops and wheels around as CORTEZ *touches his breast-plate and all half-draw their swords, clinking.*

MARINA. Hernando!

CORTEZ. You've angered the monsters, Señor!

XICOTENGA. You would not dare harm my person . . .

CORTEZ. A Christian wants to harm no one! (*To* ALVARADO *who comes in carrying a cannon ball.*) Ah, Pedro, put it here. This, Señor, is called a cannon ball.

ALVARADO *puts down the ball, the King staring at it . . .* CORTEZ *pats it . . .* ALVARADO *takes position at entrance.*

A thousand fighters sleep in here, waiting for my command. I have a hundred like this. At a word they will dig a hole in the ground the size of a tree, or tear a cloud and bring rain, – or break the back of a nation. Shall I awaken them Señor, – or may I pass through to Montezuma?

XICOTENGA (*eyes wide, he turns from the ball*). I will attack . . .

Galloping of the horse outside. Involuntarily he wheels around towards the doorway.

CORTEZ. Do I pass or do I not!

XICOTENGA (*quickly turns back to him . . . frantically*). I will attack!

CORTEZ. Wake up a thousand troops and by the one god Jesus Christ, – let them speak! Alvarado – the signal.

ALVARADO *raises his arm. Cannons boom close by.* XICOTENGA *claps his hands over his ears and sinks down in obeisance.*

XICOTENGA. Tonatiuh! Tonatiuh! (*Breaks off into incoherent mumble.*)

CORTEZ. What is he saying?

MARINA (*tears in her eyes*). He is calling you . . . the sun.

CORTEZ (*smiles. Bends and lifts him to his feet*). Lift up your
eyes, foolish King.

The King does.

Do you understand?

XICOTENGA. Have mercy on me . . . whatever I possess is
yours . . . take whatever you need . . .

CORTEZ. Send your troops away.

XICOTENGA. Let me give you some . . .

CORTEZ. I? What use have I for troops?

XICOTENGA. Do me the honour, I beg you, take ten
thousand, they will fight with you . . .

CORTEZ. But they would be afraid of Montezuma . . .

XICOTENGA (*pause*). No . . . with you, they would battle
even the Aztec. They would be honoured . . . I beg
you . . .

CORTEZ. Well . . . they'll probably be an encumbrance, but
if they would enjoy the fight, I'll accept . . . say . . . two
thousand five hundred men.

XICOTENGA. From my heart, deep thanks. Now, will you
let me go and explain to my people . . .

CORTEZ. You are free to move as you please. You will return
here in the morning.

XICOTENGA. I will bring you ten loads of fine things to eat.

CORTEZ. Good night, Your Majesty.

XICOTENGA (*a smile dawns on his face*). When Montezuma
hears of this, he'll not smile.

CORTEZ. No, he'll not smile.

XICOTENGA (*going*). It will be . . . a great year in Mexico.

CORTEZ. Aye, a great one.

XICOTENNA. *stands smiling at the thought of it, bows and
moves out facing* CORTEZ. . .

(*When* XICOTENGA *is at the door,* CORTEZ *shouts*

suddenly.) But if there is treachery, Señor, the ground will open under you!

XICOTENGA. Believe it, there is honour still among mankind.

He bows and goes out. Everyone peers out after him to make sure he's gone, then all rush at CORTEZ *roaring, congratulating him, slapping him on the back, etc. except* MARINA *who stands aside watching unhappily.*

ALVARADO. Gods! That's what we'll be! – The Sun, by Jesus!

All roar laughing.

CORTEZ (*jubilant*). And see that we act like gods! From tonight, the Spaniard is God in Mexico! Now, go out to your men, explain what has happened, but! – No drinking! We are austere. And in the morning, we march westward with legions behind us! The road is clear to Montezuma! Until dawn, Señores.

ALL (*going*). Good night, sleep well, thank God . . . (*etc.*)

CORTEZ. Sleep well. And thank you. Good night. (*To* OLID) Oh, Cristobal. It was a blunder, Cristobal . . . eh?

OLID (*going*). You're a very lucky man, Hernando Cortez.

CORTEZ. Yes. And you are not. Good night.

ALVARADO (*indicates the departed* OLID, *and with infinite pleasure*). How bitter is the gall! Lucifer himself never fell so hard and so fast as Cristobal de Olid! Sleep well, Hernando!

Both laugh as he turns to go.

Hey!

Searching around him wildly.

CORTEZ. What?

ALVARADO. My girl! . . .

CORTEZ. Even with a rope tied round your ankle, Pedro!

ALVARADO (*rushing about*). Who did it! . . . (*To* MARINA.) Did you see her!

CORTEZ. Look in your pocket!

ALVARADO. My death! What was her name! (*Rushes out.*)

CORTEZ (*laughs until he turns and sees* MARINA *who is alone with him*). He'll discover some day that you're the culprit and it will not go well with you.

MARINA. A beast should sleep with cows not children. He always finds a child.

CORTEZ. Ahh . . . I'm tired, Marina. Help me out of this . . . (*off with his breastplate.*) What do you suppose Montezuma looks like?

MARINA. A man. Like you.

CORTEZ. Handsome?

MARINA. So they say.

She goes and spreads out a blanket.

CORTEZ. And will *he* believe that Gods are walking in his state?

MARINA. I pray he does not.

CORTEZ (*laying down*) Why?

MARINA. Hernando, how will you ever break a lie when it's grown so large?

CORTEZ. When we've conquered, only the truth will reign. Believe in me, Marina!

MARINA. Tell me this, I know the others, but you – was it God or gold that brought you here to Mexico? Look in my eyes, Hernando!

CORTEZ (*pause*). Aye, there's gold in it, and a good many things that an empire's made of . . . but by my conscience, Marina, the Christ is in it too, and as deep, I think, as any other thing. (*He has her hand, pulls on it, she resists.* Believe it, Marina, I swear it to you! Come, here beside me. (*She lies down beside him, and he leans over, kisses her. Softly.*) We'll live in golden palaces, and drink from golden cups, and you shall be a golden queen, rubies in your hair, and from o'er the sea the Kings of the world will come to do obeisance at your feet . . . Marina, . . . you're weeping again. I love you child . . . look at me. Why are your eyes so dead to me. I love you, believe it . . . stop crying! . . . Stop it! You'll not leave me! Marina, I need you! Smile to me! Marina, you can't go away . . . I need you, Marina. Smile to me! There – that's better.

She smiles slowly, the tears in her eyes. He laughs suddenly, and buries his face in her breasts . . . as the lights dim out.

Oh, my dear woman, you will thank Cortez all the days of your royal life!

Scene Three

In the tower of the great Temple in Tenochtitlan, the tall figures of the two chief gods face each other: the peaceful QUETZA-COATL *on the left and* HUITZILPOCHTLI, *the God of War on the right. Before the latter, stirring a steaming cauldron which is set on a tripod, is* PARACH.

PARACH (*alone*).
Stir, stir in thy bed of evening clouds,
Descend, descend, O Huitzilopochtli God of War,
O Battlemaker, possess again the King's faint
heart,
Strike from his arms the chains of peace
That are breaking his honour as a bone.
O Lord of War, the Emperor is beguiled
By a vision that corrupts his powers.
Descend, Thunderer, burst upon the earth
Brilliant in arms! Walk again thy restless form
Into the living flesh of the Montezuma King!
Stir and descend, stir and descend . . .

He recedes from the God and approaches QUETZALCOATL
on the left. To QUETZALCOATL.

I pray you, Lord of the Wind, forgive me, Quetzalcoatl.
You blew down the flame and returned the moon
And I know it; And I know your power; I confess
I have not led the King to favour you these years
But I will change and feed you flowers once again
Abandon your revenge, O Peaceful Heart,
He is coming now to compare the Spaniard's helmet
With yours, and when he sees how unlike they are
Trick him no more, and let him destroy the Spaniard.
I will honour you again, I will not forget you
In the Years to come. . . .

Enter MONTEZUMA, GUATEMOTZIN, CAGAMA, *and*
CUITLAHUA. MONTEZUMA *carries the helmet.* PARACH
bows. They stand centre, looking up at QUETZALCOATL.

Welcome my Lords to the Great Temple of Tenochtitlan.
MONTEZUMA (*he stands a little ahead of them, without turning
from the God*). What is your prayer, my Lords?

Pause.

CUITLAHUA. It will come to be.
GUATEMOTZIN. It will never be.

Slight pause.

MONTEZUMA. And Cagama?
CAGAMA. My mind is filled with garrisons and marching
men. But compare the helmets. I should like to see.

PARACH *mounts the* QUETZALCOATL *God.*

MONTEZUMA. O Evening Star, if I beguile myself now,
instruct me . . . let this other world begin tonight, or send
me warring on the earth again! Descend, Parach, and
bring me the helmet of the God.

The Lords watch with breathless attention as PARACH *removes the God's helmet. He descends, hands it to* MONTEZUMA *who compares it with the Spanish helmet and his hands suddenly fly up and the helmets bound down the stone steps. He stands as though frozen, hands in air. Below, after a silence,* PARACH *picks both of them from the floor, Lords look at them and turn startled as* MONTEZUMA *slowly descends. As he nears the bottom . . .*

(*Softly.*) Parach? Are they not the same? Cortez's helmet and our loving God's?

PARACH (*blankly, dazed*). A god returns, but in other ways . . . a god . . . a god returns but surely not like this.

He walks into the shadows mumbling.

MONTEZUMA (*pause. With his eyes on the helmet*). Leave me now, my lords. Go to the treasury. Take two loads of gold. Precious stones. Assemble an embassy. Go to Cortez; in my name . . . welcome him to Mexico.

They don't move.

Shall I do battle with stars because a history is written and I am at the end of it? (*Silence.*) Welcome them now . . . I'll remain in fasting here for two days until they arrive. I'll be sure then, I will plunge into my soul, I'll not let them into the city until I'm sure . . . Send heralds through the empire; proclaim a state of prayer. Go, my lords – I will speak with the gods tonight.

GUATEMOTZIN. The people will see danger . . .

MONTEZUMA. Then tell them that I will never betray them to mortal man, but neither will I by impious haste unloose on them the anger of heaven.

Pause.

CUITLAHUA. May the gods bless your fast, my Lord.

MONTEZUMA. And your journey to the Spaniard. Farewell.

They bow and all go out, right.

Alone in the Temple, he stands between the gods. Turns from
HUITZILPOCHTLI *to* QUETZALCOATL.

Great God Quetzalcoatl, I am not afraid. Though you
come burning cities and mocking my name, I pray your
return. Aye, though I must walk from the throne and
treasured gold, from an empire of cities into the desert,
though the price of your returning is an impoverishment
to this robe on my back, I would be ready. But even as I
scented every wisp of wind for signs, the final augury I
knew would come not from without, but from within my
heart, and search it now, there is no singing here. Why,
am I not struck dead with such doubting in my breast?
Perhaps this is but a metal that by some dark coincidence
matches your very own? O Tranquil God, do I mock
myself! The Spaniard bleeds and dies, – when did a god
die? And they were seen eating maize! And yet, what
army of men could endure what they endure and live?
And yet, they . . . and yet, and yet, and yet! I cannot
yield an empire for a turning in bronze! I'll not give away
a people to conquerors! Plant a word in my heart! Speak
now in thunder, call through the lightning. (*Shouts.*) It is
time for a word! O Eastern Star, oh God of the gentle
heart, in what darkness shall I seek for thy word . . . !

Slow curtain as he speaks.

ACT TWO

Scene One

The sunlit rooftop of the temple. TALUA *alone, looking excitedly off into the distance, the history under his arm. Enter* MONTEZUMA *and* LORDS *and* TECUICHPO. *All dressed magnificently. The King wears golden sandals, a brightly striped toga, from his shoulders hangs a great chain of gold, fabulously engraved, his golden crown, the shape of the pontifical tiara flashing the light.* PARACH *stands beside him. As they enter,* TALUA, *unable to restrain himself.*

TALUA (*pointing out*). They're turning down the avenue, my Lord! – coming this way!

TECUICHPO. Look Father how their metal throws back the sun!

MONTEZUMA. How cautiously they move.

TALUA. And those marvellous animals? See! – sparks, their feet are filled with sparks! My Lord, a boy told me the brown ones can talk!

PARACH. Be quiet Talua.

CUITLAHUA. That must be Cortez on the white one.

CAGAMA. His back is like a spear!

MONTEZUMA. You're certain, Guatemotzin, all the garrisons are prepared?

GUATEMOTZIN. We could attack this moment!

MONTEZUMA (*pause*). Cagama, your people are ready?

CAGAMA. We could cut them down like grain, my lord.

GUATEMOTZIN. Uncle, I beg you, let me bring two thousand down the causeway from Chapultepec, five thousand over the lake from Coyoacan and we've got them in between!

MONTEZUMA (*pause. He moves nervously*). I'll meet him . . .

we have nothing to lose.

GUATEMOTZIN. But you sat two days before the gods and no word came. Look, here come the Tlascallan marching with the Spaniards! We fought them a hundred years and now they walk into the city! You cannot permit this, Uncle!

MONTEZUMA (*more uncertain*). Cuitlahua, you have men at the drawbridges.

CUITLAHUA. No one can leave the city now.

GUATEMOTZIN. My lord, look how silently the people wait in the doorways. They would bless you to let them fight!

PARACH (*looking out*). Look there! Those must be their priests. They bring a new god, not ours!

GUATEMOTZIN. Uncle, give me the golden word and I'll slaughter them where they stand!

MONTEZUMA. I cannot attack before I know.

CAGAMA. They're cut off, we've got them . . . !

MONTEZUMA. I'll hear no more! Wolves could take them now and hungry coyotes might find some honour in it! But (*touches prophecy in* TALUA's *hand*) we have our God's prophecy, my Lords, his promise of peace and wisdom on the throne of the world. You will not smash that down before I know the word the Spaniard brings!

TECUICHPO. Father, they're stopping. A woman is with them! Look! – she's dark!

GUATEMOTZIN (*all looking out, he explodes*). Oh, if it's all a mirage of words! – my Lord, who will have tears to weep for you!

MONTEZUMA. Guatemotzin, I'll not hear this again; I need no custodian for my honour. I will fight when time is for fighting.

TECUICHPO. A few of them are coming this way . . .

MONTEZUMA (*glances below*). Come – we greet the Spaniard not with the grinding teeth of barbarians, but with the confidence and smiles of our great inheritance. My Lords, we shall descend to greet them . . . let them know our race!

Exit all but TAPAIA.

TAPAIA. From the cloudless heights he descends . . .
From the black holes of the earth they climb . . .
To touch hands on a path of flowers.

> *Enter the Aztec company from the left, descending the bottom
> steps of the Temple and turning into the court, then from the
> right, the Spaniards, the path of flowers connecting both
> parties.*

> CORTEZ *flanked by* FR. OLMEDO *and* MARINA, *followed
> by* ALVARADO, ORDAZ, MONTEJO, DE LEON *and* DE
> OLID. *Part way down the flower path they stop. They all
> bow.* CORTEZ *comes forward with* FR. OLMEDO *and*
> MARINA. CORTEZ *makes a sweeping bow before* MONTE-
> ZUMA, *stands erect.* MONTEZUMA, *with simple ease, goes
> to him, stands a moment looking at his face, and from his
> shoulders he takes off the golden chain, holds it out.*

> CORTEZ *takes it, puts it on.*

MONTEZUMA. I welcome you to Mexico.

CORTEZ. Your Highness, in the name of the one God, the
Son, and the Holy Ghost . . . creator of the turning
heavens and maker of man, by the hand of my most
Catholic master Charles, I bring you greetings and most
fervent wishes for your health and boundless prosperity.
A token of our friendship, my Lord (FR. OLMEDO *takes
out a large string of glass beads.*) . . . From my brothers
and myself, these imperishable beads!

> CORTEZ *takes the beads and starts to put them over*
> MONTEZUMA's *head.* MONTEZUMA *starts back.* MARINA
> *takes the necklace quickly and holds it out by her fingertips.*
> MONTEZUMA *takes it, puts it on.*

MONTEZUMA (*fingering the beads*). I have never seen such
stones . . . what are they?

CORTEZ. Glass, your Majesty. Sand, water and sun. They are imperishable.

MONTEZUMA. And . . . where does your . . . your world . . . lie?

CORTEZ. Far to the east and beyond the sea, my lord.

MONTEZUMA (*indicating officers*). And these are your brothers?

CORTEZ. Brothers, your Majesty, under our Lord Jesus Christ.

MONTEZUMA (*to* MARINA). But the woman is one of my subjects, are you not?

MARINA. I am a Christian, great Lord. I have always dreamed of seeing you . . .

CORTEZ. Marina has guided our journey, your Majesty. She is the first of your Christian subjects – the first to see the light of the one true God.

MONTEZUMA (*pause*). You have splended eyes, Cortez.

CORTEZ. My Lord, they but reflect the Majesty of so magnificent a prince.

MONTEZUMA (*pause*). Tell me, Cortez . . . why have you come to Mexico?

CORTEZ (*pause*). Your Excellency, the question reveals a largeness of mind.

MONTEZUMA. The matter has occupied my thoughts. Why are you here?

CORTEZ. Let me be candid. My God and divine Master was heavy of heart that so mangificent an empire as your own should dwell without the blessings of our Lord, Jesus Christ. And nothing would suffice but I must carry the word of God to your Majesty and your people. For this purpose I have Padre Olmedo here – my holy man – and his brothers, who live only for the hour when they may bring you to baptism and open the gates of heaven to your princely soul. For this, my lord, I am here in Mexico. I bring you your own true God.

MONTEZUMA (*looks from* CORTEZ *to the officers, to* FR.

OLMEDO, *nods*). I should like to speak with your holy priest.

FR. OLMEDO. I am honoured, your Majesty.

MONTEZUMA (*smiling*). As for myself, you have doubtless heard wild tales of my opulence, how I dwell in golden palaces and feed emeralds to birds, and other such nonsense . . .

MARINA (*laughs*). We were taught that your eyes are made of gold.

MONTEZUMA. Only my eyes? I am usually gold from head to foot! (*They laugh.*) No, as you see, I am flesh and blood, and my city is stone and wood.

CORTEZ. But a marvellous one, my lord. When we topped the final mountain peak and saw this city on the lake below, we felt we had truly climbed into the clouds and some holy vision sparkled before our eyes.

MONTEZUMA (*flattered and happy*). It is no vision, but I do think you will find it as beautiful as I do . . .

CORTEZ. I am most anxious to see it all, your Majesty. In Cempoala they said one could buy everything in the world in your market-place.

MONTEZUMA. Ah . . . the market-place! (*Glances smiling at his Lords.*) There is a sight for your King to see. It will be open tomorrow . . . I shall send you guides to lead you. Go with your Spaniards, see the thousands of canoes glancing in and out of the canals bearing the wealth and cargo of my state. And be at ease with the people, walk with the crowds in the pleasure of the abundance that flows up from my market-place. And be sure to look in on the artists. You will find the crouching potters and jewellers from Cholula, the goldsmiths from Azcapozalco, the hunters from Xilotepec, and the painters are sometimes there from Tezcuco. Every art and article of my people will lie open to your eyes. Tapestries are sold, and cotton – spun and in bales, dresses for women, and coverlets too, and in cages are animals of every kind and colour, wild and tame, – Cortez, I – I wish I could take you by the hand and show you my city!

CORTEZ. Your Majesty, I shall remember this hour forever . . .

MONTEZUMA. I think we shall have happy days, Cortez. And soon you must tell me of *your* world? We shall . . . (*laughs*) . . . exchange wonders.

MARINA. They bring a gentle God, my Lord . . . the greatest wonder.

MONTEZUMA. But now . . . you must need rest . . . My steward will show you to my old palace.

CORTEZ. Most generous, Montezuma.

MONTEZUMA. I have but one request. Your Tlascallan allies . . .

CORTEZ. Not allies, your Excellency, – followers. They will all be Christians soon.

MONTEZUMA. Nevertheless they cannot be quartered in the city.

CORTEZ (*smiling, but stubbornly*). It will be hard to give them that news, my Lord . . .

MONTEZUMA. I regret the necessity. We have been at war with Tlascalla this sheaf of years, and my people despise them. Send them to the outskirts.

MARINA. That would be best, Hernando.

CORTEZ (*slight pause*). As you wish, my lord.

MONTEZUMA. I shall be pleased to receive you tonight. And bring the holy man with you . . .

FR. OLMEDO (*obsequiously. Holds his crucifix*). Will it please your Majesty to receive this into your hand?

MONTEZUMA. What is it?

MARINA. The crucifix – sign of Jesus Christ . . . it will help you to understand, great Lord.

MONTEZUMA *looks at it carefully, then reaches out and takes it.*

FR. OLMEDO. My Lord, you hold in your hand the key to

the riddle of the Universe . . .

CORTEZ (*jubilantly*). Your Majesty, no traveller in any age was ever blessed with such a journey's end . . . ! I embrace you in . . .

He suddenly goes to embrace MONTEZUMA, *who quickly cries out and steps back in horror as* GUATEMOTZIN *and* CAGAMA *push* CORTEZ *away. Two Spaniards rush in and there is a scuffle for a moment.*

(*To* ALVARADO, *who is violently pushing* GUATEMOTZIN *away from him*) Pedro, stop!

Silence. Both sides stare shocked at each other.

MONTEZUMA. . . . I am never touched.

CORTEZ (*relaxes*). Oh, my lord, I meant only to embrace you in friendship – a thousand, thousand pardons. I beg you, forgive me!

MONTEZUMA *is at a loss for what to say.*

Farewell, your Majesty . . . until tonight.

He waits for some word, but there is none. He bows, the Spaniards bow, back out along the path, turn and go out into the roadway and disappear. TAPAIA *bows to* MONTEZUMA *and follows them. The Lord and the King watch the empty entrance way in silence.*

TECUICHPO (*frightened*). Father . . . how fierce their eyes became!

MONTEZUMA. The key to the riddle of the Universe!

MONTEZUMA *looks at the crucifix in his hand, the Lords look at it.* MONTEZUMA *turns towards the stairs, consternation on his face, and as he mounts the stairs with* GUATEMOTZIN. . .

GUATEMOTZIN (*noticing something out beyond the wall*). Uncle . . . look . . . The city . . . the city is empty!

MONTEZUMA. . . . Where are the people? Where are *my* people? (*Astonished.*)

He turns quickly to the crucifix in his hand; as though it held the reason for the empty city; and he quickly goes up, turning it in his hand.

The stage darkens.

Scene Two

About two weeks later on the rooftop of the Temple. This is the highest point in the city, – a flat platform ending on the right in the top few steps of the stairway up the side of the building, and on the left leading into the entrance of the Temple Tower. Overhead a clear sunlit sky.

Discovered are CAGAMA, CUITLAHUA, *and* PARACH *intently looking down the stairway at something far below. Silence a moment, then all turn about as* MONTEZUMA *hurries from the tower with* GUATEMOTZIN.

MONTEZUMA. How do you interrupt me at prayer?

GUATEMOTZIN. My Lord, Cortez is climbing up with his troops.

MONTEZUMA. Troops? He said nothing about bringing troops.

GUATEMOTZIN. Will you come and see for yourself, my Lord. (*Leads the King to the platform's edge and points below.*)

PARACH. They'll curse us all with their impudence.

GUATEMOTZIN. Do you see them, my Lord? Two weeks and they walk the city like masters.

CAGAMA. I think it is time they understood their welcome is ended . . .

MONTEZUMA (*hesitates, then returns from the edge*). They must not be antagonized. They understand they are to leave soon. He asked to visit me here.

CUITLAHUA (*indicating below*). But what does this mean? Troops . . .

As he speaks, TECUICHPO *enters from around the front of the tower, and gradually makes her way to the edge.*

MONTEZUMA (*impatiently*). What do you think it means, brother? Is the city to be attacked now by such a brigade?

GUATEMOTZIN. But how do we know . . .?

MONTEZUMA. You are too quick to distrust them! I have not yet heard all Cortez has to say. (*Turns to* PARACH.) He's come to see the statues of our sacred Gods.

PARACH (*astounded*). You'll bring them *into* the temple . . . ?

MONTEZUMA. Jesus Christ is not a stranger there I think.

PARACH. How can you say such . . . ?

MONTEZUMA. Listen when Cortez speaks; you might be wiser now. Christ like Quetzalcoatl walked the earth as a man, he cured the sick and like the white god He promised to return one day . . .

PARACH. I see it in your eyes; you're turning from our gods!

MONTEZUMA. Or searching for them?

PARACH. In Cortez?

MONTEZUMA. Perhaps. There is a hint of God in Hernando Cortez's eyes, something I feel we must touch and if we do, it will lift us up. (*To* LORDS.) I also see the danger, but . . . be patient. Come, Parach.

He goes into the temple tower, PARACH *follows him, shaking his head.*

CUITLAHUA (*reverently*). How his thoughts fly heavenward. A priest-king!

GUATEMOTZIN. Aye, but if they're mocking him – (*Turns suddenly and shakes his fist towards those below . . .*)

CUITLAHUA (*looking down*). Who are those two coming up?

TECUICHPO. The tall one is Alvarado.

GUATEMOTZIN. Your eyes are uncommonly sharp, Tecuichpo.

TECUICHPO (*smiling*). Alvarado is an uncommon Captain.

GUATEMOTZIN (*turns full to her*). Indeed, my love.

TECUICHPO. Yes, and if my lords would leave me to greet him . . .

GUATEMOTZIN. Alone?

TECUICHPO. Oh, he'll not harm me if I let him talk. (*Smiles.*) The Captain loves to talk.

GUATEMOTZIN. Have you spoken to him before?

TECUICHPO. Last week when father took me to visit them. Alvarado is quite human.

GUATEMOTZIN. Well!

TECUICHPO. . . But not Cortez. Cortez never talks about himself.

CUITLAHUA. Let her talk to him, Guatemotzin.

GUATEMOTZIN. But alone?

TECUICHPO. Please, Guatemotzin, leave me with him. Sometimes a woman . . . can see in the dark. (*She looks up at him into his eyes. He lifts her hand and kisses it.*) Hurry. They're coming.

All the LORDS *hurry into the tower. Above, she strolls a little to the left, smoothing her gown. Enter* ALVARADO *and* LEON. *Her back is turned to them.*

ALVARADO (*puffing, happily surprised on seeing her alone. Bows*) Ah, Princess!

TECUICHPO (*turns suddenly as though surprised*). Oh!

ALVARADO. I am only Captain Alvarado.

TECUICHPO. It is a long climb from below.

ALVARADO. Depending on who is at the top, Princess. I may say you are even more lovely by day than by night.

TECUICHPO. Thank you, Captain. And is this Captain Sandoval?

LEON. De Leon, Princess. (*To* ALVARADO.) We have a message to deliver.

ALVARADO. Let me deliver it alone, Leon.

LEON. But . . .

ALVARADO. By your love for me, Leon.

LEON. I know, but . . . Princess, will you tell your father . . .

ALVARADO. Gonzalo! (*Turns slowly to her, bows.*) Excellent lady, we bear a communication from our beloved Cortez, Señor Hernando Cortez. He desires to inform his Majesty, the Emperor, that he has come for an audience. Will my lady be so kind as to notify her father?

TECUICHPO. Your words fall like feathers through the air.

ALVARADO. You may trust the Princess to deliver the message.

LEON. But Hernando is waiting . . .

ALVARADO. Señor?

LEON (*shakes his head*). Oh, Pedro, Pedro . . .

He turns and goes down the stairs.

ALVARADO. My comrade has no poetry.

TECUICHPO. But he knows his duty.

ALVARADO. But I love to talk to you. I am so far from home, gentle lady. Have you ever been far from home?

TECUICHPO. No, but I should like to see your country.

ALVARADO. Spain would kneel at your feet. I am famous in Spain, you know.

TECUICHPO. Are you? And is Cortez more famous?

ALVARADO. Well . . . yes. He is famous too, but my father was Commendador – a Lord as you say.

TECUICHPO (*trying the word*). Commendador.

ALVARADO. Say it again, please?

TECUICHPO. Commendador.

ALVARADO. Your lips *embrace* a Spanish word! – Say my name.

TECUICHPO. Alvarado.

ALVARADO. Princess . . . your voice is the sound of Spain. (*Moves closer.*) Have you ever heard how I swam three miles in full armour?

TECUICHPO. You must be very strong.

ALVARADO. I broke a crocodile's jaw with this arm. Feel it.

TECUICHPO (*touches his forearm*). Like iron, Captain.

ALVARADO (*looks in her eyes*). You . . . have never heard of the crocodile?

TECUICHPO. I . . . I'll tell my father you've come . . .

She draws from him.

ALVARADO (*takes her arm*). . . . . Say my name again. I have not heard a woman say it in so long.

TECUICHPO. Alvarado.

ALVARADO. Your voice . . . is Christian.

TECUICHPO. And I?

ALVARADO. You are the most beautiful woman I have ever seen.

TECUICHPO (*pause*). And . . . what are you?

ALVARADO. I? (*Pause.*) I am a man. A Christian man.

TECUICHPO. Is that more than a man?

ALVARADO. Is a man more than an animal? It is a man with God in him.

TECUICHPO (*pause*). I'll give my father your message.

She starts left, he snatches her hand.

ALVARADO. Gentle girl . . . will we meet alone again?

TECUICHPO (*smiles, frightened*). We may, Captain . . . Alvarado.

ALVARADO. Oh, my heart!

He tries to embrace her, she pushes him away.

TECUICHPO (*a hushed shout*). Please! . . .

Enter CORTEZ and other Captains up the stairs.

CORTEZ. Pedro!

ALVARADO *breaks from her.*

(*Bowing*) My deepest apologies, Princess.

She turns about and rushes inside.

CORTEZ *goes to* ALVARADO.

CORTEZ (*hushed*). Are you mad? Are you *mad*? This is a temple! A holy place!

ALVARADO. I have been eating too much meat.

CORTEZ. Am I announced or is your brain altogether addled?

ALVARADO (*a little dazed*). She's gone to tell him now. Oh, Hernando, what a jewel to pin a sheet with!

CORTEZ. You'd better see to your duty, Captain. Come here, Señores.

Captains gather round him.

(*To* ALVARADO.) Now do as I tell you, Alvarado. (*Motions below.*) Burn that scene into your eyes. I want the exact position of every drawbridge on every causeway . . . throw her out of your mind.

ALVARADO. I'll have it, I'll have it.

CORTEZ. Remember, you'll draw a map of it when we're back in quarters. You, Señores, form a circle around Pedro, but at ease. The King is very suspicious. (*To* ALVARADO.) Precise now, Pedro. We may live or die by this. The drawbridges are the windpipes of this city. See you know where they are – exactly.

ALVARADO. I will, Hernando.

CORTEZ. Marina, tie up my sandal?

She bends to it.

Spread out now, Señores. At your ease.

ALVARADO. A crucifix on this height could be seen for miles around.

MONTEJO. A fairy white city in the heart of heathendom.

It never seemed so white from below.

CORTEZ (*restlessly glancing at the tower doorway*). Why does he keep us waiting like this?

FR. OLMEDO. Hernando, I am beginning to think we're moving too fast.

CORTEZ. Too slow, Padre. We're here two weeks with nothing accomplished.

MARINA *finishes with his sandal, he walks away.*

. . . nothing . . .

MARINA. You're too impatient, Hernando. We've made friends with him . . .

CORTEZ. I did not leave Spain to make friends with Montezuma. What does he mean by this?

MONTEJO. Another polite hint to go home, I think.

CORTEZ. Treachery, he's famous for it.

MARINA. It's a grave decision for him to make. Unbelievers are never allowed here in the temple.

CORTEZ. I am tired of hearing what is allowed and what is not allowed!

FR. OLMEDO (*softer*). Hernando, be reasonable. Is it good judgement to insist on converting such a heathen in sixteen days?

CORTEZ. Is it better judgement, Pedro to wait until his weathercock brain decides we're devils come to destroy his Gods?

FR. OLMEDO. Your fancy is running away with you.

CORTEZ. Fancy! Is it my fancy, or have we been served inedible food these last three days? Have the servants been rude or have they not? Montezuma is turning against us, Padre. Believe it.

ORDAZ. Aye.

MARINA. I don't believe it.

LEON. You don't believe anything.

MARINA. And you don't understand these people. They live to brood. And if we're being told to leave now, we deserve no better.

CORTEZ. And what does that mean?

MARINA. He gives you a palace to live in, the finest to eat,
and drink, servants, women – kings could ask no more,
and what do you do? You curse him for a heathen . . .

CORTEZ (*ignoring her*). Montejo, go down and tell them to
keep a sharp eye up here.

MONTEJO *goes down.*

MARINA. Hernando, you must change your ways or . . .

FR. OLMEDO. I say we go down.

CORTEZ. We are going inside, Padre.

FR. OLMEDO. Zeal is warping your judgement, Hernando.

CORTEZ. Zeal, zeal! (*Strides about.*)

FR. OLMEDO. A superstition as black as his is not thrown
off in two weeks.

CORTEZ. I've seen it thrown off in an hour!

FR. OLMEDO. By threats! With a knife held over them!

ORDAZ. He's had time enough to understand Christ. Too
much.

MARINA (*to* ORDAZ). *You* have blood in your eyes, Ordaz.

FR. OLMEDO. Hernando, for the sake of his soul, stop
forcing Christ on him.

CORTEZ (*wheels about*). Understand me, Padre. We are not
safe in Mexico until Montezuma is Christian.

FR. OLMEDO. But so quickly! The man is not a peasant . . .

CORTEZ (*out of patience*). Padre. I beg of you understand
me. It is no longer a question of Montezuma's soul. He
must brood no longer under the claws of that priest of his,
or he'll hatch a vulture to devour my heart . . . if he's not
doing it already.

FR. OLMEDO. I can only tell him the truths . . .

CORTEZ. You can bring him faster to baptism.

FR. OLMEDO. In time . . .

CORTEZ. There *is* no time! On the day you are Montezuma's
confessor, Mexico is ours, and not until then.

FR. OLMEDO (*sighs*). I'll try my best.

CORTEZ. More, Olmedo, you will save his soul today or we are parted from ours tomorrow!

FR. OLMEDO. Trust me, Hernando.

CORTEZ. I do, but remember this as you love your life; we are no Gods, – he'll know it soon, and when he does he'd better be a Christian convert or we'll be walking with the Holy Ghost.

Cocks his ear towards the doorway.

(*Low to* ALVARADO.) Take care, Pedro, he's coming. Remember, Señores at ease.

Enter MONTEZUMA, plus GUATEMOTZIN, CAGAMA, CUITLAHUA *and* TECUICHPO. *All bow, saying, 'My Lord . . . Majesty . . . ' etc.*

MONTEZUMA. I hope you are not weary climbing so high.

CORTEZ. Spaniards are never weary, my lord.

MONTEZUMA (*pause. He turns to* ALVARADO). Are you Alvarado?

ALVARADO. Captain Pedro de Alvarado, your Majesty.

MONTEZUMA (*looks closely a moment, turns to* CORTEZ). I have glad news for you, Cortez. My priest will permit you to see the Gods.

CORTEZ. I am most grateful, my Lord. I would hardly know how to excuse myself to my master if I failed to see them.

MONTEZUMA. Then you are leaving us soon?

CORTEZ (*slight pause*). Quite soon, your Majesty.

MONTEZUMA. But not today.

CORTEZ. Oh no, my Lord.

MONTEZUMA. Because I have so much to ask you.

CORTEZ. I enjoy a question, my Lord.

MONTEZUMA. But tell me, what will you say of my city when you see your Lord?

CORTEZ. Why . . . I will describe its beauties, and its . . .

MONTEZUMA. But what *exactly*? Sometimes, Cortez, I fear

you are more polite than enthusiastic.

CORTEZ. An injustice, my Lord. As I have said before, there are great cities in my country – Burgos, Medillin, Madrid, Seville, – names that bring most graceful towers to my sight. But this, your Majesty, is to Seville as a full-bodied woman to a scrawny maid. This . . .

MONTEZUMA. No, you must make a picture for his mind. Here . . . (*Takes* CORTEZ *to the right upstage corner.*) Tell your King . . . say . . . say . . . Montezuma's city is a woman and she floats, white and clean, on the rippling waterface, bathing her sides on an inland sea (*As he speaks*, ALVARADO, *who is downstage, motions for the* CAPTAINS *to shield his back, and takes out a piece of paper and sketches what he sees below, at a furious pace.*) . . . and her hair is forty fountains that wave with the sunlit breeze. And tell him of the palace with the sweetwood ceilings and the cedar walls. And the aviary too where the birds are kept . . . tell him of the birds. And the hospital there where the sick are tended, and the avenue, Cortez, where forty men may walk abreast . . . and the House of Wild Animals . . . tell him what you see.

GUATEMOTZIN *appears out of the shadow downstage of the tower. He watches* ALVARADO.

CORTEZ. My Lord, I will tell him that Montezuma's city surpasses Rome, and Rome as I have told you, is the seat and glory of the world.

GUATEMOTZIN *springs forward, snatches* ALVARADO's *paper.*

ALVARADO (*as the paper is snatched from him*). Hey . . . !

He goes for GUATEMOTZIN *as* MONTEZUMA *and* CORTEZ *rush downstage.*

CORTEZ. Pedro . . . !

ALVARADO (*trying to wrest the paper from* GUATEMOTZIN).

Give me that paper . . . !

MONTEZUMA. What has happened . . . !

CORTEZ. Let him go, you fool! Did you hear me, Alvarado?

They break apart. GUATEMOTZIN *examines map. Enter* CAGAMA *and* CUITLAHUA *and* TECUICHPO *quickly.*

MONTEZUMA (*glancing at* ALVARADO). What is that, Guatemotzin?

CORTEZ. Pedro, what did you do . . . ?

GUATEMOTZIN. The captain is an artist, my Lord. Look.

Hands map to MONTEZUMA.
MONTEZUMA *examines it, his face hardens, he seems to expand.*

CORTEZ. What is it, my Lord?

GUATEMOTZIN (*to* LORDS). This one draws a map and he dares ask what . . . !

CORTEZ. A map! Captain, did you draw a map?

ALVARADO. It's a lie, I never . . . !

CORTEZ. There must be an error . . .

MONTEZUMA (*restraining himself by laughing*). Many, yes . . . I looked upon a man and saw a God, and you took a King for a fool!

CORTEZ. Let me explain . . . !

MONTEZUMA. Explain, explain! Or do Christians save an emperor's soul with a military map!

CORTEZ. I ordered no map drawn so it is not a map!

MONTEZUMA. What is it then – the plan of that other world you brought me from the sun? Why have you come to Mexico, Cortez?

CORTEZ. Well, my lord, since I am convicted as a villain there is nothing more to say . . . (*Angry*). But I would never have believed that the Aztec state could see danger in three hundred and fifty mortal men!

MONTEZUMA. Danger? I see no danger; only mockery, –

but it ends now! What do you want in Mexico?

CORTEZ. Want? I want another heaven here, I want a way of life in Mexico that Jesus Christ will bring, I want a country where men will live not in revolt against a righteous king but as brothers on the earth, – aye, my Lord, I want nothing here but the brotherhood of man, and I crossed the sea to lay it in your hand!

Enter TAPAIA.

TAPAIA (*breathless*). My lord . . . !

MONTEZUMA. What is it?

TAPAIA. A courier from the coast: a new army . . . a thousand Spaniards have landed! (*The Spaniards freeze.*) The commander says he'll arrest Cortez on sight as a rebel to his own King!

MONTEZUMA *turns to* CORTEZ, *his eyes moist.*

CORTEZ. Pay them no attention, my Lord . . .

MONTEZUMA. Oh, we are diseased . . .

CORTEZ. I will attend to them, they're bandits, the lowest of the low, they . . .

MONTEZUMA. 'My lord, I want another heaven here . . .'

CORTEZ. They have no right to come here . . . !

MONTEZUMA. 'Men will live as brothers on the earth . . . '

CORTEZ. They're traitors, they . . . !

MONTEZUMA. Traitors? Out of that other heaven? *I* have traitors, *I* have mortal enemies, but I rule by force and not the brotherhood of man!

CORTEZ. Let me . . . !

MONTEZUMA. Leave me! The map is drawn and Christian curses Christian . . . and man is still man!

He turns and starts into the temple.

CORTEZ (*threateningly*). You misunderstand me, Montezuma.

MONTEZUMA *turns about slowly.*

CORTEZ. I cannot leave Mexico until you are Christian.

Pause.

MONTEZUMA (*points out around the horizon*). There are twenty-two cities around this lake and eighty thousand troops who would bless me to end this in blood! Begone!

CORTEZ. I will not leave your soul for the fires of Hell! Be Christian or by the wrath of Jesus Christ, I'll crash the heavens down upon your head!

MONTEZUMA. You leave the city by tomorrow sunset, and in three days if there is a Spaniard left on the soil of my Empire, he'll die on it!

CORTEZ. Emperor, I pity your soul!

MONTEZUMA. Out of my sight!! – a *man* I can kill!

CORTEZ *turns and goes down followed by all the Spaniards and* MARINA. MONTEZUMA *and the* LORDS *quickly to the ledge and look down.*

CAGAMA (*undertone*). Pull the drawbridges . . . ! Cut them off!

GUATEMOTZIN. Fall on them now . . . let me signal the garrisons . . . !

MONTEZUMA. We will not attack until tomorrow sunset . . .

CUITLAHUA. They'll never go without a struggle! They never will!

MONTEZUMA. I promised peace until tomorrow . . .

CAGAMA. But *they* promised nothing!

MONTEZUMA. Let them go!

GUATEMOTZIN. We could bury them in arrows now!

CUITLAHUA. The armies are ready, why should we wait!

MONTEZUMA. You're changed, brother!

CUITLAHUA. Yes, I stand with Cagama and Guatemotzin.

MONTEZUMA (*walks from them, shaking*). Stand? Against

what do you stand?

CUITLAHUA . . . against nothing, my Lord.

MONTEZUMA. Then you stand for the standing's sake!
(*Almost weeping.*) I saw another world . . . a world where
every door stood wide unbolted in the night, where the
single ear of corn grew heavy as a child, and all the brass
of war, swords and shields, were melted into rivers and
the silver sea . . . into the sunrise . . . Let them walk
away. I cannot bring my hand to kill them yet. (*He looks
at each one, then testingly.*) Good day, my Lords.

They don't stir.

(*With a note of command and warning.*) Good day, my
lords!

Slight pause, then they bow stiffly and start to go.

(*Stronger.*) He will suffer who lifts an arrow before I
command.

The LORDS *are immobile, silent.*

I say they are not molested, my lords!

They avoid his eyes.

Am I unworthy of an answer!!

Slight pause.

GUATEMOTZIN. Your honour and your state will be
defended.

MONTEZUMA *searches their eyes. Nods.*

MONTEZUMA. Leave me.

LORDS. My Lord, great Lord!

They bow and go down the steps. He is alone with
TECUICHPO.

MONTEZUMA (*stands quietly a moment*). Was ever such a fool

as Montezuma? Such a proud and pompous fool to sit private among clouds while down below the charts are drawn to loot him while he prays!

TECUICHPO (*goes close to him*). Father . . .

MONTEZUMA. Oh, my child, my child, it was so clear, so clear in my eyes . . . !

He clasps her face and weeps, his tears buried in her hair.

Slow curtain.

ACT THREE

Scene One

The Spanish quarters in the old palace. At the left is a large wooden cross standing at the wall, a low table with papers on it and a candle.

It is a few hours before dawn. The Captains are scattered all over the floor, asleep in their armour. CORTEZ *is slowly and silently pacing back and forth deep in thought. He stops at the table looks at the papers and starts for the men as though to wake them but changes his mind. As he is resuming his pacing, he stops as though at a noise and* MARINA *hurries in and goes directly to him.*

They speak hushed.

MARINA. Hernando!

CORTEZ. Where have you been . . . !

MARINA. You've got to leave.

CORTEZ. Why? Where were you!

MARINA. When we were coming back from the Temple I heard a man in the street saying 'Guatemotzin will attend to them before long.' I followed him . . . Hernando, the priests are telling the people that a flood will come if you aren't killed at once. The Lords have broken with the King, and they're getting ready to attack you . . . !

CORTEZ. When?

MARINA. There'll be an uprising if you're not away tomorrow! Go now . . . !

CORTEZ. Ssh!

He quickly goes to ALVARADO *and prods him with his toe.*

Up! Up! – Wake up, Pedro.

ALVARADO (*violently lashing out flies up to a sitting position*).
Take it out! Take it out, you . . . ! Oh . . .

MONTEJO. Heh? What? What?

LEON (*jumping up*). What's happened?

CORTEZ. Wake up! Wake up!

He goes to the table and examines the papers.

ORDAZ. It's the middle of the night.

OLID. Who made that noise?

ALVARADO. I dreamed I walked up to Panfilo Narvaez and
his thousand men and broke his neck in my hand.

LEON. Where were you all night, Marina?

CORTEZ (*for quiet*). All right, all right! Quiet.

ORDAZ (*scratching*). Fah! I'm lousy as the King of France –

LEON. Some day you should take a bath, Ordaz.

ORDAZ. Aye, and you . . . !

CORTEZ. Señores! Please.

ORDAZ. A foot-soldier doesn't travel on his ass so that he
can afford to drain away his strength in hot water . . . !!

CORTEZ. Gentlemen! Marina says they will attack us
tomorrow!

Slight pause.

OLID. Who? Who will attack?

CORTEZ. The Lords have broken with Montezuma!

MONTEJO. Then we must leave. . . !

OLID. What are we waiting for?

ALVARADO. Shut up . . . !

CORTEZ. Will you let me talk or must we die like idiots!
(*Silence. Goes to the table, lifts a paper.*) I have two letters.
Aztec troops attacked our garrison on the coast
yesterday, and killed Captain Escalanto.

MONTEJO. Its started . . . !

ALVARADO. I told you Montezuma is treacherous!

ORDAZ. What happened . . . !

CORTEZ. I don't know if the King ordered that attack, but this I do know, our subject towns are mumbling revolution against us, or they couldn't have persuaded a man to attack the coast garrison. Now here's another note – from the prodigy of the good governor of Cuba, – Captain Panfilo Narvaez. I read: 'You are outlaws, my dear Cortez, and I am in Mexico to bring you to justice. Either you forfeit to me all properties, and claims you have stolen, or you pay the fine in blood.'

ALVARADO. Who in hell is Narvaez to tell us . . . !

CORTEZ. Who is he? He is fourteen ships, a hundred and fifty arquebussiers, over nine hundred men, heavy guns, a thousand Cubans, eighty horses and enough ammunition to blow Madrid to the stars.

OLID. Plus the law, Hernando, which is not on our side.

ALVARADO. What law? What are you gibbering about?

OLID. Simply that we are disowned by his Majesty's officer, the governor of Cuba! (*To* CORTEZ.) Now: if you had a document from Charles . . .

ORDAZ. A fart on documents! We're here, and we bled to get here, and if stiff-necked Narvaez wants to root us out let them come and do it!

OLID. Oh, he's coming, Ordaz, and with more logic than you have . . .

ORDAZ. A fart on logic! I have too many wounds to be read out of Mexico! What's the word, Hernando?

CORTEZ. The word? We must go out and pound that bastard into submission whatever his force. Narvaez must be stopped.

MONTEJO. But we can't kill Spaniards. The Aztec would see!

ORDAZ. Let them! Once we've got Narvaez, we . . .

OLID. Yes, we're out of the city and there'll be war getting back in!

MONTEJO. We'll never get in again!

CORTEZ. Unless!

MONTEJO. Heh?

CORTEZ . . . unless we hold in our hands before we leave, such a precious thing as no Aztec will dare injure us for fear of injuring it! (*Dead silence.*) Yes, señores, we can't remain here, or go away until we take Montezuma prisoner.

Silence.

MARINA. Prisoner . . . !

MONTEJO. Are you mad?

CORTEZ. It must be done!

ORDAZ (*to* CORTEZ). I'm with you, Hernando!

MARINA. The whole country would fall on you!!

ALVARADO (*to men*). How can you hesitate!

OLID. They'll wipe us out!

MONTEJO. Listen to her, she knows these people! Marina . . . !

MARINA. Hernando, you'll never . . . !

MONTEJO (*to* MARINA, *desperate*). They'd let us out peacefully, Marina, wouldn't they?

CORTEZ. Nonsense!

MARINA. Nobody would harm you if you left.

MONTEJO. There!

ORDAZ (*to* MONTEJO). Just because you're loaded with gold, Montejo – is no reason to deny others the opportunity.

MARINA (*to* ORDAZ). But, Señor, Montezuma is . . . a God would not dare touch him . . . ! Hernando, what will you do if he won't . . . if he refuses to . . . (*Breaks off seeing their faces.*)

CORTEZ. He would be worthless, dead.

MARINA. I don't care what he would be worth, you . . . you would never kill him?

Silence. Beginning to plead.

He'll be Christian one day . . . I know . . . he will . . .

(*Silence.*) Hernando, you would never kill a King!

CORTEZ. No more words. We must decide, Señores.

MARINA. I don't understand, what will you decide?

CORTEZ. That's enough, Marina!

MARINA. But he'll be Christian if you let him . . . !

CORTEZ. Shut your mouth!

Makes to strike, she recoils.

MONTEJO (*nervously*). I don't see it. That's all, I don't see it.

LEON. I think perhaps . . .

MONTEJO. She says they'll let us out and we ought to go! It would be another matter if, for instance . . . (*Sound.*) What are you doing removing the cross?

CORTEZ *is moving the cross out of the niche in the wall. They come up slowly one by one behind him,* MARINA *with them.*

CORTEZ. When Taurez, the carpenter, carved out the altar here, he found a door behind the plaster. I shall open it, Señores, but as you love me, keep secret what you see.

He pushes open a stone door in the wall. They peer inside, blocking MARINA's *view. One comes away with a audible gasp, another jumps to fill his place.*

LEON. El Dorado . . . !

MONTEJO. There must be a million pesos worth . . . !

MARINA. What is it, let me see! (*She is blocked.*)

ORDAZ. All the gold in the world! (*To* MONTEJO.) Well, Montejo, are you still rich enough?

MARINA *is looking in, carefully.*

MONTEJO. It must be one . . . no three billion pesos worth! Let me feel it in my hands!

He starts to go into the compartment as MARINA *turns about quickly, and bars the way with her body.*

MARINA. No! What have you done?

MONTEJO. Out of my way . . . !

MARINA. It is a tomb! (*Silence.*)

CORTEZ. What is happening to you, Marina?

MARINA. These things are never touched . . .

CORTEZ (*angering*). But what is becoming of you!

MARINA. This is sacred, Hernando, the heritage of all the Aztec kings, their crowns, their clothes are buried here.

CORTEZ. There's more in there, more than all the Kings of Europe own!

MARINA. The vilest thief would never dare to violate . . . !

MONTEJO. We're going in, Hernando!

VOICES. We'll have it . . . ! Tell her to get away! (*Etc.*)

CORTEZ (*goes to her with an embrace*). Marina, why do you . . .

MARINA (*repelling him*). No. This can never belong to you. In there . . . is Mexico.

CORTEZ. Let them go in.

MARINA (*slight pause*). Hernando – will you desecrate a tomb?

CORTEZ. Leave!

MARINA *looks at him for a moment, then goes. He strides to her and swings her about.*

Where are you going?

MARINA. I'll tell him, I'll break the lie to the King . . . !

CORTEZ *slaps her across the face.*

Hernando . . .

She half stumbles away from him. He snatches at her, she tries to go on.

CORTEZ. Where!! (*Grabs her arm. Into her face.*) Where are you going!! Where! Where!

He hits her to the floor.

We have two hours until dawn, Señores. Rest till

sunbreak; I will send word to Montezuma that I am visiting; while I am talking to him Avila has twenty five men sauntering into the palace in two's and three's. Leon sees that the remainder of the army is in the courtyard and surrounding the palace in the streets. As soon as we take him, I leave to deal with Narvaez and . . .

MONTEJO. We'll die at it, I know we'll die!

CORTEZ (*shout*). We'll take him! – and without a blow . . . I know that man.

Scene Two

Next morning in the throne room. MONTEZUMA, *with* QUAUHOPOCA, *commander of the Tuxpan garrison. At his feet is a round leather box.*

MONTEZUMA. I still see no excuse, Commander. You had no order from me to kill Spaniards.

QUAUHOPOCA. I never dreamed Cuitlahua would issue a command without your consent.

MONTEZUMA. You were not trained to take commands from my brother.

QUAUHOPOCA. The word was on all lips that you were moving to war.

MONTEZUMA. Do you command my Tuxpan garrison by rumour now? (*Noticing the box.*) What is in this box?

QUAUHOPOCA. The head of the Spaniard, Juan de Escalante, my lord.

MONTEZUMA (*his eyes fastened to the box*). Let me see.

QUAUHOPOCA (*opening the box*). He branded the faces of women . . .

Begins to lift the head out.

MONTEZUMA (*turns his eyes*). Take it away.

QUAUHOPOCA. You never used to quail at dead things.

MONTEZUMA. Take it out of the city, and don't offer it to any God, – they're leaving today . . . you should never, never have done it!

Enter TAPAIA.

TAPAIA. Your daughter has come, my Lord.
MONTEZUMA (*not listening*). Very good, Tapaia.
TAPAIA. There is something I cannot understand, my Lord.
MONTEZUMA. Yes?
TAPAIA. A great many Spaniards have been seen coming into the palace.
MONTEZUMA. Naturally, Cortez is coming to say farewell.
TAPAIA (*resolutely*). A guard should be here with you . . .
MONTEZUMA. I am not at war. Let Tecuichpo enter.

TAPAIA *bows and goes out.*

(*To* QUAUHOPOCA.) Wait outside, Commander.

QUAUHOPOCA *picks up box.*

I am expecting Cortez. If he wishes to question you, answer him and only with the truth.
QUAUHOPOCA. I had never expected I should be accounting to a Spaniard for my actions.
MONTEZUMA. You will do as I say, Commander.
QUAUHOPOCA. To the last of my days.

Enter TECUICHPO.

QUAUHOPOCA. Princess . . .

Exit QUAUHOPOCA.

MONTEZUMA. He has grown very insolent.
TECUICHPO. You summoned me, my Lord?
MONTEZUMA. Come here, daughter. (*Embraces.*) You know, that Cuitlahua, Guatemotzin and Cagama have not attended me since yesterday.
TECUICHPO. Yes, father. Old Tapaia told me.

MONTEZUMA (*pause*). Guatemotzin left no word with you where he might be found?

TECUICHPO (*sadly*). No, I have not seen him since he left yesterday.

MONTEZUMA. You would not tell me an untruth?

TECUICHPO. He left me no word, father. Why do you not send a call out for him?

MONTEZUMA. I have sent out more than a call. If he is found he is under arrest.

TECUICHPO. Arrest . . . !

MONTEZUMA. Guatemotzin is a traitor. And my brother and Cagama too, – all traitors!

TECUICHPO. But they mean only to defend you . . .

MONTEZUMA. I am still able to decide when I need protection and when obedience. Guatemotzin is rousing the people against my laws and will suffer for it.

TECUICHPO. How will he suffer, father?

MONTEZUMA. You are about to weep.

TECUICHPO. Yes, I am about to weep.

Pause.

MONTEZUMA. Your tears will not help him. I have borne the last of his disobedience.

TECUICHPO. You will not harm Guatemotzin, Father.

MONTEZUMA. You may go.

TECUICHPO (*a frantic cry*). You must not harm him, Father.

MONTEZUMA. Leave me!

TECUICHPO (*weeping as she shouts*). Always a reason to pardon the Spaniard; – pardon their sacrilege, pardon their murders, pardon their fingers that creep for my body, but the anger is quick for the princes who worship you . . . !

MONTEZUMA. Traitors who mock me . . . !

TECUICHPO. Go then, – find Guatemotzin, run him down like a thief for the love that he bears you, – but seek for no mourners when your blood runs out!

MONTEZUMA. Daughter . . . !

TECUICHPO. Has your skin turned white that you persecute friends and honour your enemies?

She rushes from the room as he reaches out for her.

MONTEZUMA. Tecuichpo!

He stands still facing the doorway, then covers his eyes.

My child.

Enter TAPAIA. *Stands a moment.*

TAPAIA. My Lord?

MONTEZUMA *is silent.*

Cortez is here.

No response.

My Lord, will you look down into the courtyard? (MONTEZUMA *mechanically turns and goes towards the window.*) There are seventy of them. They have no baggage for travelling.

MONTEZUMA (*turns angrily*). How dare he mobilize such numbers inside the city! Call him here!

TAPAIA. Would it not be wise to remove your daughter from the palace my Lord? – in case of violence in the streets . . .

MONTEZUMA. There will be no disturbance, Tapaia.

TAPAIA. The people are angry my Lord, and now with these Spanish soldiers . . .

MONTEZUMA. Very well. Take her to the Temple.

TAPAIA. And let me summon you a guard, my Lord?

MONTEZUMA (*annoyed*). Have you lost your senses? Who ever dared touch me? Go; I'll see the Spaniard.

TAPAIA. At once, my lord.

Exit TAPAIA.

MONTEZUMA *looks slowly at the courtyard, then goes to the throne and sits on it slowly, perturbation on his face.*

Pause. Enter CORTEZ, MARINA, ALVARADO, ORDAZ, LEON *and* MONTEJO. *All bow saying 'My lord, Majesty,' etc. All men needed.*

MONTEZUMA. I am honoured, Captain, but I gave no permission for such a massing of men before the palace!

CORTEZ. I regret that I found it necessary to bring so many soldiers for my protection.

MONTEZUMA. Protection?

CORTEZ. Your Majesty. From the very first instant of my entrance into Tenochtitlan I ordered my Captains to do all in their power to help and serve you, – but you have done exactly the opposite for us.

MONTEZUMA. The opposite? I have done everything . . .

CORTEZ (*louder, fiercer*). I am astonished, your Majesty, astonished, that after declaring yourself my friend you should stoop so low as to order your garrison at Tuxpan to take arms against my Spaniards.

MONTEZUMA. I never gave that order . . .

CORTEZ. You murdered my brother!

MONTEZUMA. It is not true! You're mistaken . . . !

CORTEZ. Juan de Escalante dead is no mistake, Montezuma! I demand that those responsible be apprehended and severely chastised.

MONTEZUMA (*pause*). As for chastising my officers, Cortez, I am the one to decide that. And as for my ordering the slaying of your captain, you must accept my word I was ignorant of the order.

CORTEZ. I do accept your word, but I will only be convinced when you bring the guilty parties from the coast for my questioning.

MONTEZUMA. I am happy to give you that opportunity now. Will one of you go into the outer room and call Commander Quauhopoca?

CORTEZ. What does this mean?

MONTEZUMA. He is the commander of my Tuxpan Garrison.

CORTEZ (*waves his hand impatiently*). I have no interest in seeing him now.

MONTEZUMA. But surely you want the truth?

CORTEZ (*stands boiling with rage. With an angry jerk of his hand, his teeth clenched, he glances at* LEON). Bring him in then Leon.

MONTEZUMA. You will *call* him in.

Exit LEON.

I am afraid, Captain Cortez, that you have given ear to the tales of my enemies.

CORTEZ. I give ear to no tales, I know truth from falsehood . . .

Enter QUAUHOPOCA *erect as always, proud to the set of his lips.*

MONTEZUMA. Commander, this is Captain Hernando Cortez. (COMMANDER *bows stiffly.*) Captain, is there something you would like to ask him?

CORTEZ (*swaggers up to* QUAUHOPOCA, *speaks two inches away from his eyes*). So this is the man who murdered Juan de Escalante?

QUAUHOPOCA. I murdered no one. Your man was killed in battle.

CORTEZ. But you attacked, did you not!

QUAUHOPOCA. I am not spoken to in such a fashion.

CORTEZ (*shouting*). By my beard but you will be!

MONTEZUMA. He will not! He is not to be shouted at, Cortez. He is . . .

CORTEZ (*over-riding*). Did you attack my garrison at Villa Rica?

QUAUHOPOCA. I attacked your garrison and your man was killed.

CORTEZ. From whom did you receive the command to march?

QUAUHOPOCA. From my Lord Cuitlahua, the Emperor's brother.

CORTEZ (*bursting*). But you knew, of course, that Cuitlahua could give no command without the Emperor's consent?

QUAUHOPOCA. This time the order was without his consent.

CORTEZ. Am I to believe that you, a garrison commander, will move your troops without knowing first whether your Emperor approves?

QUAUHOPOCA. What you believe is of no interest to me!

MONTEZUMA. Quauhopoca, you must answer the Captain.

QUAUHOPOCA. I have given him the truth, my Lord, but I do not think he will be satisfied with it.

CORTEZ. No, not with your kind of truth. You tell me you killed Escalante on Cuitlahua's orders. Will you tell me which sovereign you serve?

QUAUHOPOCA. What other sovereign could I serve, but Montezuma?

CORTEZ (*suddenly*). Your Majesty, I must speak with you alone.

MONTEZUMA. Wait outside, Quauhopoca.

QUAUHOPOCA *bows and exits.*

CORTEZ. Do you not have a guard for him?

MONTEZUMA. My soldiers need no guards to detain them. So you see, Captain, you were too hasty in putting the crime on me.

CORTEZ. I see nothing of the sort.

MONTEZUMA. You heard the Commander . . .

CORTEZ (*venomous crescendo*). I heard the Commander, and I heard too that your army is running wild killing Spaniards, knowing only the authority of their own beastly lust! Do you expect me to depart when there is such disorder in the country? Do you think me blind not to know that your own nobility is holding secret consultations seeking my annihilation?

MONTEZUMA. There are troops out at this moment to arrest my rebellious lords. You will not shout at me, Captain.

CORTEZ (*pause. He walks from him, the blood pounding in his head. His hand is on his sword, his jaw out-thrust*). My dear Majesty, it is apparent to me, despite my fervent wish, that you have not the slightest intention of giving *my* sovereign the satisfaction of a fair hearing!

MONTEZUMA. Fair! Why, Cortez . . .

CORTEZ (*shouts*). I see it!!

MONTEZUMA (*with the shout; the impact of unreasonable, relentless force hits him. He scans the captains*). What is the point of this? What do you want here? Cortez, what do you want?

CORTEZ. Your Majesty, I do not wish to begin a war over this matter, and it would grieve me if I had to destroy this lovely city; which I assure you, I could do at a moment's notice. But your conduct has been such that I no longer feel my soldiers are safe while you are left to your own devices unsupervised by Spaniards. Therefore, your Majesty, I am willing to forgive your crimes against me and your treachery a thousand times manifested, only if silently, and without raising any disturbance, you will come with us to our quarters where you will be served and honoured as you are here . . .

MONTEZUMA *emits an inarticulate sound.*

CORTEZ . . . but cry out and you will die!

MONTEZUMA (*slowly, as though pressing his fears behind him, he rises from the throne*). I am not the person to whom such an order can be given.

ALVARADO. You're wasting words on this son of a bitch! Seize him, and if he resists, swords in his guts!

All whip out their swords.

MONTEZUMA (*the clang on the metal forces him back a step*).
You dare not . . .

CORTEZ *points his sword at* MONTEZUMA's *heart and
begins to advance.*

MARINA (*rushes to* MONTEZUMA). Go with them! They will
treat you with honour! They'll kill you, otherwise, they
will, I know it!

MONTEZUMA. You dare not do it! I am Montezuma . . . do
you hear me, I am the Emperor! . . .

CORTEZ (*prods him up against the wall*). Lower your voice,
Señor! You will not go as prisoner, but as the Emperor
changing his residence from one palace to another.
(*Pause.*) Well? What is your decision?

MONTEZUMA. They will come from Cholula, out of
Xilotepec, from the corners of Empire destroying the
world, they'll tear out your hearts!

CORTEZ. Out with the word, Montezuma! – or I will murder
you myself!

MONTEZUMA (*his hands raised, the sword at his heart, he
searches the helmetted faces around him. His voice choked
with hatred, sadness and the humiliation of his hour*). I will
go with you.

CORTEZ (*thrusts sword back in scabbard. Makes to embrace
MONTEZUMA*). Majesty!

MONTEJO *runs out.*

MONTEZUMA. Do not touch me.

CORTEZ. We must be friendly now, my lord. It was all God's
will.

MONTEZUMA *looks senselessly at* CORTEZ.

(*To* ALVARADO.) Pedro, I leave for Narvaez.

ALVARADO. With victory, Hernando.

CORTEZ. And those of you that remain, remember, Captain
Alvarado's word is my word, and he who disobeys it will

answer to me! (*To* MONTEZUMA.) You will be given every courtesy and if there is one thing wanting I will appreciate your reporting it to me when I return. However, should you be tempted to join in any movement to incite rebellion; you will be the first to fall by my sword. I repeat, the slightest suspicion of treachery will push a swordspoint through your heart!

MONTEJO *approaches with chains and manacles.*

MONTEZUMA (*dumbly*). Chains? There must be no chains.

CORTEZ. Only until . . .

MONTEZUMA. I cannot have chains on my body.

CORTEZ. They will be removed in a little while when you go to our quarters. Come, Señores, you that are coming. Marina?

MARINA. Why must you chain him, Hernando?

CORTEZ. Marina, there is no time for this.

MARINA *goes to* MONTEZUMA, *curtsies low; goes out without raising her eyes.*

SEVERAL. God bless you, Hernando! Farewell . . . (*Etc.*)

CORTEZ (*to* ALVARADO). Pedro? (*Silence.*) The arm is strong, but the touch is light. Farewell . . . Montezuma.

Exit CORTEZ, LEON, SANDOVAL. *Silence.* MONTE-ZUMA *stares blankly at them.*

ALVARADO. The irons, Montejo.

As they take the chains out of the bag, ORDAZ *goes to* MONTEZUMA, *lifts the gold chain he wears from his neck. And while the ankles and wrists of the king are being shackled . . .*

ORDAZ. I will take your necklace, sir, or it might get stolen. How beautiful! You know, if your people had the sense for religion that they have for fashioning gold, your country would be the first in the world . . .

MONTEZUMA (*with a roar, he flings his half-chained arms in the air*). My Lords!! Guatemotzin!! Oh, my country, forgive me . . . !!

ALVARADO. Stop his mouth! (*They do so.*) That's better. Now the chains. Hands and feet my boys.

MONTEZUMA *weeps*.

Scene Three

The boom of the cannon from close by. The curtain rises on the Spanish quarters. On the left the large cross is pushed aside; the door of the concealed room open, and near its entrance is a great ornamented case overflowing with the treasure, – heirlooms and gold pieces of art of all kinds. Strewn about the floor and cloths, feathers, etc., ripped off the objects leaving only the gold.

CAPTAIN DE OLID is at this work; digging about in the case, fetching up a piece, ripping off all non-gold, and giving the remainder to MESA; who stands over a cauldron and dumps in the booty.

ARBENGA is busy with a long-handled mould which he dips into the cauldron, fills, lifts out, dips into a bucket of cold water, and opens over a neat pile of gold bars on the floor near Centre. They are working feverishly when stage lights up, as though impelled by the cannon outside and the noises of war. There is no sound from them until ARBENGA, after adding a bar to the growing pile.

ARBENGA. At last, his Royal Majesty, the King of Spain has his name stamped on Montezuma's gold. (*Chuckles, counts bars.*) Uno, dos, tres, quatro, cinco . . .

OLID. Arbenga!

ARBENGA. I'm only counting, Captain. I love it.

OLID. You'll wear them down with all your counting. Get back inside and fetch out more gold to be melted down.

ARBENGA *returns to his work.*

MESA (*stirring the cauldron*). But we're dying of thirst. Oh, if gold could turn to water for one minute.

OLID. You'll have water enough as soon as we get out of here. Now Mesa, we melt gold – as much gold as we can.

MESA (*lifts ladle high, pours molten gold before his tongue*). By the Good Mary, I'm dry enough to drink it down.

ARBENGA. And when we're back in Castile you can show them how to piss pesos!

They laugh as CORTEZ, ALVARADO, MONTEJO, ORDAZ, LEON *quickly enter.*

OLID. Señores! Hernando, you've returned, thank God.

CORTEZ (*goes straight to gold pile*). Is this all?

OLID. The cauldron took time to heat.

CORTEZ. Keep at it a little longer. But hurry, Olid. (*Notices gold pitcher on floor.*) What is this pitcher?

OLID. I am keeping that out.

CORTEZ. Everything goes in . . . Everything.

OLID (*grabs it from him*). No! It is too beautiful, Hernando.

CORTEZ (*slight pause*). Oh, very well. How much longer can the south wall hold them off, Ordaz?

ORDAZ. Maybe . . . twenty minutes, twenty five.

CORTEZ. And the west section, Montejo?

MONTEJO. I'll hold it.

CORTEZ. What is your opinion, Alvarado?

ALVARADO. We'll hold them off if they're not reinforced again.

Agreement – pause.

CORTEZ. Leon, bring Montezuma here.

LEON. He refuses to move.

CORTEZ. Refuses! Then drag him by the ears! Now! We

must crack this siege!

Exit LEON.

(*Directed at* ALVARADO, *with anger*.) The King is changed since I left, Pedro, we must talk now. (*Turns to Captains*.) To your posts, Señores! And Montejo, tell Sandoval that his corner gun is firing too high. Go, Señores, the siege is broken in twenty minutes and we are out of here.

Exit MONTEJO *and* ORDAZ.

Well, Pedro, I am ready to listen. What started this uprising?

ALVARADO. Treachery, it was all treachery, Hernando.

CORTEZ. But the reason? – and I tell you it had better be good!

Off the thundering step of a hurrying man. Enter Señor Panfilo Narvaez, fat, a patch over his right eye, a spade in his hand.

NARVAEZ. I'll not suffer this a moment longer!

CORTEZ. To your post, Narvaez!

NARVAEZ. To treat me like a groom! I, Panfilo de Narvaez, they force me to dog for water! The Governor will hear of it, Cortez, I warn you!

CORTEZ. Señor Narvaez, if I have to listen to another outburst from your Excellency, I'll rip out your left eye as I did your right!

NARVAEZ. Ha! So this is how you subdued this country! (*Mimicking*.) Montezuma is my vassal! – Oho! A Spaniard can go from one end of the country to the other without a sword! – Oho! They'll break through your devil-damned walls in a moment!

CORTEZ (*whips out sword*). Señor?

NARVAEZ (*backing away*). His Majesty will hear of this!

He'll . . . what's this? My God, Cortez . . . !

CORTEZ. Yes, Panfilo . . . there's enough gold on this floor to buy every pig in Europe to stuff your fat gut with.

NARVAEZ *laughs greedily.*

Get back to your post now!

Exit NARVAEZ.

ALVARADO. There goes the devil's ass.

CORTEZ. Well, I'm waiting – what started it, Pedro?

ALVARADO. Everything was all right till the day before yesterday when we burned that bastard Quauhopoca before the palace.

CORTEZ. I hope Montezuma had approved the death sentence.

ALVARADO. Oh, he did, yes. The people were disturbed by the burning, but I paid little attention to that because we were holding Montezuma. Well, yesterday I'm petitioned to allow one of their religious festivals in the Temple court. I give them permission providing there was to be no human sacrificing and no arms carried. They agree. Then I find out that all the heads of the noble families are to take part; and they are going to carry concealed arms, and it is not to be a religious celebration at all, but a signal for an uprising. I wait until they are all assembled last night, let them begin the dancing and the music, and then we fell on them leaving not one of them alive. In one hour the city is in revolt, and we are under siege. There is the truth, Hernando, by my honour!

CORTEZ. I heard it another way, Pedro.

Silence.

CORTEZ. You never received information about a signal for insurrection.

ALVARADO. Hernando! They carried arms!

CORTEZ. Then show me those arms! (*Roars.*) By Blessed

Mary, where are they?

ALVARADO *is silent*

I'll wager though you can show me the gold trinkets you robbed from the bodies after the slaughter. You looted their best men before their eyes, and now we're bleeding.

ALVARADO. Very well . . . if you call me liar . . .

CORTEZ. You're a fool, Pedro. You've conducted yourself like a madman!

Enter MONTEZUMA *brought in by* LEON *and soldiers.*

MONTEZUMA (*off*). I do not want to see him. His voice still wracks in my ears!

CORTEZ. Is this the value of your pledge? – to besiege my Spaniards as soon as I turn my back?

MONTEZUMA. I would have been honoured to have led the attack.

CORTEZ. You wretched dog of a King! . . .

MONTEZUMA (*sees the gold processing*). What is this? – (*He looks from the case to the cauldron to bars; and goes to* OLID, *grasping his wrist.*) Spaniard, you mistake your eyes . . . This is not gold you rip apart. This is Mexico you plunder here, not gold. (*Lifts out bracelet.*) Look, what will this bring? – but an Emperor wore it on his arm . . . and here, a featherweight of gold, but lines of Aztec Kings were nourished from this cup . . . my father's sceptre! Don't, don't throw that in . . . !

Sound: a loud hiss.

Cortez . . . you are melting down a history, are you wise enough for that! Man! – we are nothing but these dead bars . . . is this your Christian art I failed to understand?

He cries out – scuffle.

CORTEZ. Stop him!

MONTEZUMA. Let me burn with the rest!

CORTEZ. Keep him tied up and hurry . . . on with the work quickly! Melt down as much as you can.

Enter ORDAZ *running.*

ORDAZ. They've fired the sheds on our side of the east wall.

CORTEZ. Montezuma, it is within my power to blow up your city and leave it in ashes . . .

MONTEZUMA. You will die in those ashes . . . !

CORTEZ. Señor, be assured that before I do, not a stone will be left standing in Tenochtitlan. I will call off the fighting if you will speak to your people now, and tell them to open a path for us out of the city.

MONTEZUMA. You had not reckoned with such bravery in Aztecs, did you, Cortez?

CORTEZ. I did not reckon with such treachery!

MONTEZUMA. Bravery, captain, say it! Say it, Spaniard!

CORTEZ. Yes . . . they are very brave.

MONTEZUMA. Then they are not fool enough to hear Montezuma again.

CORTEZ. They still respect you, they'll listen.

MONTEZUMA. May the Gods forbid it.

CORTEZ (*shouting*). I'll smash every building into dust! I'll destroy their city forever!

MONTEZUMA. I believe you! I will go, I will go to my people. For the sake of the living who are about to die, and the dead whom I betrayed. For love of a city unparalleled on earth before, I go to my city, and if you live to see your King again, tell him how you beguiled an Emperor, but do not omit how you bent your knee before his betters, the people of his state.

Turns quickly, goes out, followed by soldiers, and as CORTEZ *follows . . .*

CORTEZ. Olid, haste, haste, Olid . . . melt everything.

Exit CORTEZ.

*They continue with the gold-melting at an even faster pace as
. . . the light fades.*

Scene Four

*The roof of the great temple moments later. The booming of
cannon and sounds of war seem to come from the streets below.*

*Curtain up on the rooftop empty. The sky overhead is grey with
approaching rain.*

MONTEZUMA *enters followed by* CORTEZ, ORDAZ, ALVAR-
ADO, MONTEJO *and* SOLDIERS. *From the group a* DRUM-
MER *steps out to the ledge and beats out an insistent roll while a*
SOLDIER *appears next to him holding high a white banner.
Gradual silence below.* DRUMMER *stops.* MONTEZUMA *steps
from the group to go to the ledge, and it is perceived that*
MONTEZUMA *has a short-sword at his back. He turns to*
CORTEZ.

CORTEZ. Raise the banner. Let them see the sign.

Drum begins again, reaches crescendo, hushed silence below.

Your Majesty, speak to the people!
MONTEZUMA. With your sword in my back, Conquistador?
CORTEZ. In case there is still treachery in you. Speak to
them!
MONTEZUMA. My people, it is late for Montezuma to be
coming from his house with words for his countrymen.
But I see in your eyes a question: What does Montezuma
have in his heart that he speaks now? What more will he
take from us, this King who holds council with
murderers? – I want nothing from you; I speak not to be
obeyed, but to plead with you. I come no more the golden
Montezuma on his royal way, I am but an Aztec man

who would preserve his countrymen from further butchery . . .

GUATEMOTZIN (*from below*). You led us to butchery, Montezuma! – you!

Shouts of assent.

MONTEZUMA. Guatemotzin, I hear your voice, and I am grateful.

Pause.

It is better that I lose your love than I should hear you weep for me and forfeit up your spirit. And I speak to you, Guatemotzin, and you, Cuitlahua, my brother who stands with arrows, and you, Cagama, and to all the rest – noble men who could not bide with vassalage, and you, Tenochtitlan, my fearless city, hear me. You have met the conqueror with thunder on his tongue, and you have conquered him. You, the mixer of lime, the breaker of stone, the scribe, the hawker of wares, you have conquered the conqueror, who came to enslave you.

CUITLAHUA. The Spaniards continue to fight! They will not be conquered, until we kill them all!

MONTEZUMA. They continue to fight because they cannot bear to die unless the city be buried with them! (*Pause.*) Believe me, my country, I ask no mercy for them. But if this war goes on there will be no stick of wood unburned in Tenochtitlan, and no family spared. You have been valiant, – generations shall sing of your valour, but is it valour now or folly to destroy what is yours uncontested and safe? (*Pause.*) I ask you then, I, Montezuma, the king without right to ask of you the dust of your feet! – We must not live out our lives among ashes! People of Tenochtitlan . . . lay down your arms!

Silence below.

GUATEMOTZIN (*a furious shout*). O base man!!

MONTEZUMA (*raises his arms*). Guatemotzin, let the Spaniards depart.

GUATEMOTZIN. Base Aztec.

Great cry of anger from below.

CAGAMA. Woman!

CUITLAHUA. Coward!

CAGAMA. The white men have made you a woman!

A roar of anger below – flights of arrows.

MONTEZUMA (*raises arms quickly, as though to ward off a blow*). No, brother . . . !

Scream of terror.

No!!

CORTEZ. Shield his body!

Before the Spaniards can shield him, MONTEZUMA *is struck and falls into a Captain's arms.*

CORTEZ. He's hit! Carry him inside, Alvardo! – Hurry! The rest follow me.

Disappears unsheathing his sword. ALVARADO *lifts MONTEZUMA to take him inside the temple.*

ALVARADO. Your Majesty? I will find someone to come and tend your wounds.

ALVARADO sets MONTEZUMA *down, goes toward the stairway. Silence – left, out of the shadows,* TALUA, TAPAIA *and* TECUICHPO *furtively appear.* ALVARADO *stops a distance from the princess. All stand awaiting his move. Presently,* ALVARADO *bows.*

TECUICHPO (*running forward*). Father! Father!

ALVARADO. Princess.

MONTEZUMA. Tecuichpo! . . . Captain . . .

ALVARADO. She is safe, Señor. (*To her.*) While I am gone,

be kind to your lovely face. (*Snatches her to him and kisses her roughly.*) Buenas Noches, Señorita . . . I will dream of you.

He runs up the stairs and disappears.

TECUICHPO (*tears streaming*). Oh Father . . .

MONTEZUMA. Where have you been, Tecuichpo?

TECUICHPO. Hidden here in the Temple. I will find medicines.

MONTEZUMA (*takes her hand*). No. Stay.

TAPAIA. You bleed, my lord, let me find surgeons.

MONTEZUMA. I am beyond surgeons, old man. Tapaia, you must take her to safety . . .

TECUICHPO. Where? Where shall we go?

MONTEZUMA. To Guatemotzin's city. (*She weeps.*) Aye, we have come the full circle.

TECUICHPO. Let me stay with you, Father . . .

MONTEZUMA. No, no . . . take her, Tapaia, and when the Spring is come to Mexico again, let there be a great wedding. And in the day of that glory, let not the halls of Guatemotzin's house hear my name.

FR. OLMEDO. Let me touch your head with holy water . . .

MONTEZUMA. Oh, false, false priest. Take your holy water, Cortez, and drown your sins; I am not so fallen that a serpent can bring me into grace.

FR. OLMEDO *rises slowly.*

CORTEZ. For the last time, I beseech you renounce your idols and open your way into heaven.

MONTEZUMA. And you Captain? Will you go to heaven?

CORTEZ. When I have made my last confession.

MONTEZUMA. If there is a God who will forgive you your sins, Hernando Cortez, you betray me again, for your God is bloodier than mine. There could have been a time when I would be Christian. I believe it so. But now, I tell you with my remaining breath; Jesus Christ may be good above all gods; but Christians are debased below all men.

CORTEZ. Señor . . . with all my heart I beg you . . . ! Live
. . . and when I return . . .

MONTEZUMA . . . Your very steps will dig your grave and
we will rot together in the gentle earth, for when my
people struck me, I was oppression in their eyes. Look on
me, Conquistador; in my unmourned face see your face,
and in my destiny, the destiny of all oppression that dares
to dig its heel in the living heart of Mexico.

CORTEZ *starts to speak as* MONTEJO *dashes in.*

Farewell, my daughter.

They embrace.

TECUICHPO. Farewell, Father.

TAPAIA. Farewell . . . my world – come, child.

Takes TECUICHPO's *arm and they go.*

MONTEZUMA. And you, Talua? Will you not leave me? –

TALUA *stands silent, as though he will never go.*

Go then, and bring me the written history –

TALUA *bends and kisses his hand, rises and goes out through
shadows on left, through which* TECUICHPO *and* TAPAIA
have just gone.

Enter CORTEZ, MARINA, FR. OLMEDO, *carrying a
crucifix, and soliders. They enter from right quickly.* MARINA
kneels on his right side, FR. OLMEDO *on the left,* CORTEZ
at his feet; stands and looks at him a moment.

MARINA. See, he bleeds . . . find water . . .

Starts to minister to him.

MONTEZUMA. Leave me . . .

CORTEZ. Let Marina bind your wounds, my Lord.

MONTEZUMA (*tears away a bandage*). No! Away with the

medicines. Leave me!

CORTEZ. I have come so that you may be baptized in the name of Jesus Christ.

MONTEZUMA. Is my blood not enough but I must also render up my soul? You'll not have it, you'll not have it from me, though it wander lost to the end of time betrayed at every turning of the wind.

MONTEJO. They're digging under the barricades with their fingers, – we can't hold . . . !

CORTEZ. Then we break for the open streets! (*Draws sword.*) Come!

He hurries up the stairs and out; sword in hand; followed by Fr. Olmedo. Marina halts as she sees Talua coming out of the shadows, the prophecy under his arm. She watches as TALUA *slips to his knees beside the King.*

TALUA. My lord . . . The history . . .

MONTEZUMA (*long pause*). Talua . . .

TALUA. I write of this year?

MARINA *appears from the shadows, listens.*

MONTEZUMA. Write the truth, yes.

TALUA. What is the truth my lord.

MONTEZUMA (*pause*). Let the history tell how an emperor died in search of the golden years. And by no hand but his own. For while his eyes were searching heaven for meanings and signs, a sword was pointing at his breast, and as it caught the light with such brilliant glare, it seemed to hold the sanction of the sun, and he dared not turn the killing blade away. And when the sun was set, and the light was gone, the emperor felt for the face of the god but the steel stood turning in his heart.

MARINA *rushes down to him, weeping.*

MARINA. My Lord, what have I done! (*She falls to her knees beside him.*)

TALUA. He's dying, Marina.

MARINA. Why does he smile?

MONTEZUMA. Talua . . . read to me again . . . how the god shall return . . .

TALUA (*opens the stone book*) 'From out of the place where the sun comes up, warming the ocean sea . . . '

A terrific booming of cannon very close by. TALUA *is frozen.* MARINA *starts towards the stairs when her eye is caught by a helmet on the floor. She picks it up, looks tearfully at* MONTEZUMA, *and goes up the stairs as . . .*

'From out of the place where the sun comes up, warming the ocean sea, there shall come again the departed one, and with him, shining brightly from his hand, a year has come. The first of a sheaf of The Golden Years . . .'

As he reads . . . Cannon

Slow curtain.

The Man Who Had All The Luck

A Fable

CAST

DAVID BEEVES
SHORY
J.B. FELLER
ANDREW FALK
PATTERSON BEEVES
AMOS BEEVES
HESTER FALK
DAN DIBBLE
GUSTAV EBERSON
AUGIE BELFAST
AUNT BELLE

The Time   *Not so long ago.*

Act One
Scene One   *An evening in early April. Inside a barn used as a repair shop.*
Scene Two   *The barn, near dawn.*
Act Two
Scene One   *June. About three years later. The living room of the Falk's – now David's house.*
Scene Two   *Later that day. The living room.*
Act Three
Scene One   *The following February. The living room.*
Scene Two   *One month later. The living room at evening.*

ACT ONE

Scene One

A barn in a small, midwestern town. It is set on a rake angle. The back wall of the barn sweeps toward upstage and right, and the big entrance doors are in this wall. Along the left wall a work bench on which auto tools lie along with some old parts and rags and general mechanic's junk. A rack over the bench holds wrenches, screwdrivers, other tools. In the left wall is a normal-sized door leading into Shory's Feed and Grain Store to which this barn is attached. A step-high ramp leads down from the threshold of this door into the barn. Further to the left, extending into the offstage area along the wall, are piles of cement bags. In front of them several new barrels which contain fertilizer.

Downstage, near the centre, is a small wood stove, now glowing red. Over the bench is a hanging bulb. There is a big garage jack on the floor, several old nail barrels for chairs – two of them by the stove. A large drum of alcohol lies on blocks, downstage right. Near it are scattered a few gallon tins. This is an old barn being used partly as a storage place, and mainly as an auto repair shop. The timber supports have a warm, oak colour, unstained. The colours of wood dominate the scene, and the grey of the cement bags.

Before the rise, two car horns, one of them the old-fashioned ga-goo-ga type of the old Ford, are heard honking impatiently. An instant of this and the curtain rises.

DAVID BEEVES *is filling a can from an alcohol drum. He is twenty-two. He has the earnest manner of the young, small-town business man until he forgets it, which is most of the time. Then*

*he becomes what he is — wondrous, funny, naïve, and always
searching. He wears a wind-breaker.*

Enter J.B. FELLER *from the right. He is a fat man near fifty,
dressed for winter. A certain delicacy of feeling clings to his big
face. He has a light way of walking despite his weight.*

J.B. Sure doing nice business on that alcohol, huh David?
(*Thumbing right.*) They're freezing out there, better step
on it.

DAVID. Near every car in town's been here today for some.
April! What a laugh!

J.B (*nods downstage*). My store got so cold I had to close off
the infant's wear counter. I think I'll get a revolving door
for next winter. (*Sits.*) What you got your hair all slicked
for?

DAVID (*on one knee, examines the spigot which pours slowly*).
Going over to Hester's in a while.

J.B. Dave! (*Excitedly.*) Going alone?

DAVID. Hester'll be here right away. I'm going to walk back
to the house with her, and . . . well, I guess we'll lay down
the law to him. If he's going to be my father-in-law I
better start talking to him some time.

J.B. (*anxiously*). The only thing is you want to watch your
step with him.

DAVID (*turns off spigot, lifts up can as he gets to his feet*). I can't
believe that he'd actually start a battle with me. You
think he would?

J.B. Old man Falk is a very peculiar man, Dave.

Horns sound from the right.

DAVID (*going right with the can*). Coming, coming!

He goes out as from the back door, SHORY *descends the ramp
in a fury. He is in a wheelchair. He is thirty-eight but his age
is hard to tell because of the absence of any hair on his body.*

> *He is totally bald, his beard does not grow, his eyebrows are*
> *gone. His face is capable of great laughter and terrible sneers.*
> *A dark green blanket covers his legs. He stops at the big doors*
> *with his fist in the air. As he speaks the horns stop.*

SHORY. Goddam you, shut those goddam horns! Can't you
wait a goddam minute?

J.B. Lay off, will you? They're his customers.

SHORY (*turns*). What're you doing, living here?

J.B. Why, got any objections? (*Goes to stove, clapping his*
arms.) Jesus, how can he work in this place? You could
hang meat in here. (*Warms his hands on the stove.*)

SHORY. You cold with all that fat on you?

J.B. I don't know why everybody thinks a fat man is always
warm. There's nerves in the fat too, y'know.

SHORY. Come into the store. It's warmer. Shoot some
pinochle. (*Starts towards the ramp to his store.*)

J.B. Dave's going over to see Falk.

SHORY *stops.*

SHORY. Dave's not going to Falk.

J.B. He just told me.

SHORY (*turns again*). Listen. Since the day he walked into
the store and asked me for a job he's been planning on
going to see Falk about Hester. That's seven years of
procrastination, and it ain't going to end tonight. What
is it with you lately? You hang around him like an old
cow or something. What'd your wife throw you out of the
house again?

J.B. No, I don't drink any more, not any important drinking
– really. (*He sits on a barrel.*) I keep thinking about those
two kids. It's so rare. Two people staying in love since
they were children . . . that oughtn't to be trifled with.

SHORY. Your wife did throw you out, didn't she?

J.B. No, but . . . we just got the last word: no kids.

SHORY (*compassionately*). That so, Doctor?

J.B. Yeh, no kids. Too old. Big, nice store with thirty-one different departments. Beautiful house. No kids. Isn't that something? You die, and they wipe your name off the mail box and . . . and that's the ballgame.

Slight pause.

(*Changing the subject; with some relish.*) I think I might be able to put Dave next to something very nice, Shor.

SHORY. You're in your dotage, you know that? You're getting a Santa Claus complex.

J.B. No, he just reminds me of somebody. Myself, in fact. At his age I was in a roaring confusion. And him? He's got his whole life laid out like a piece of linoleum. I don't know why but sometimes I'm around him and it's like watching one of them nice movies, where you know everything is going to turn out good . . . (*Suddenly strikes him.*) I guess it's because he's so young . . . and I'm gettin' so goddam old.

SHORY. What's this you're puttin' him next to?

J.B. My brother-in-law up in Burley; you know, Dan Dibble that's got the mink ranch.

SHORY. Oh don't bring him around, now . . .

J.B. Listen, his car's on the bum and he's lookin' for a mechanic. He's a sucker for a mechanic!

SHORY. That hayseed couldn't let go of a nickel if it was stuck up his . . .

Roar of engines starting close by outside. Enter DAVID from the upstage door, putting a small wrench in his pocket. As he comes in two cars are heard pulling away. He goes to a can of gasoline and rinses his hands.

DAVID. Geez, you'd think people could tighten a fan belt. What time you got, John?

SHORY. Why, where *you* going? You can't go into Falk's house . . .

From the store enter AUNT BELLE. *She is carrying a wrapped shirt and a bag. She is a woman who was never young; skinny, bird-like, constantly snivelling. A kerchief grows out of her hand.*

BELLE. I thought you were in the store. Hester said to hurry.

DAVID (*going to her*). Oh, thanks, Belle. (*Unwrapping a shirt.*) It's the new one, isn't it?

BELLE (*horrified*). Did you want the new one?

DAVID (*looking at the shirt*). Oh, Belle. When are you going to remember something! Hester told you to bring my new shirt!

BELLE (*lifting them out of bag*). Well I – I brought your galoshes.

DAVID. I don't wear galoshes any more, I wanted my new shirt! Belle, sometimes you . . .

BELLE *bursts into tears.*

All right, all right, forget it.

BELLE. I only do my best, I'm not your mother . . .

DAVID (*leading her right*). I'm sorry, Aunt Belle, go – and thanks.

BELLE (*still sniffling*). Your father's got your brother Amos out running on the road . . .

DAVID. Yeh, well . . . thanks . . .

BELLE (*a kerchief at her nose*). He makes Amos put on his galoshes, why doesn't he give a thought to you?

DAVID (*pats her hand*). I'll be home later.

SHORY. You know why you never remember anything, Belle? You blow your nose too much. The nose is connected with the brain and you're blowin' your brains out.

DAVID. Ah, cut it out, will ya?

With another sob, BELLE *rushes out.*

She still treats me like after Mom died. Just like I was

seven years old. (DAVID *picks up the clean shirt.*)

SHORY (*alarmed*). Listen, that man'll kill you. (*Grabs the shirt and sits on it.*)

DAVID (*with an embarrassed but determined laugh, trying to grab the shirt back*). Give me that. I decided to go see him, and I'm going to see him!

Enter PAT *and* AMOS *from right.* PAT *is a small, nervous man about forty-five,* AMOS *is twenty-four, given to a drawl and a tendency to lumber when he walks.*

PAT (*on entering*). What's the matter with you?

DAVE *looks up.* ALL *turn to him as both come centre.* AMOS *is squeezing a rubber ball.*

(*Pointing between* DAVE *and stove*). Don't you know better than to stand so close to that stove? Heat is ruination to the arteries.

AMOS (*eagerly*). You goin', Dave?

SHORY (*to* PAT). Everything was getting clear. Will you go home?

PAT. I'm his father, if you please.

SHORY. Then tell him what to do, father.

PAT. I'll tell him. (*Turns to* DAVID *as though to command.*) What exactly did you decide?

DAVID. We're going to tell Mr David Falk we're getting married.

PAT. Uh, huh. Good work.

SHORY. Good work! (*Pointing at* PAT, *he turns to* J.B.) Will you listen to this . . . !

J.B. (*he shares* SHORY's *attitude towards* PAT, *but with more compassion.*) But somebody ought to go along with him.

PAT (*adamantly to* DAVID). Definitely, somebody ought to go along . . .

AMOS (*to* DAVID). Let me go. If he starts anything, I'll . . .

DAVID (*to* ALL). Now look, for Christ's sake, will you . . .

PAT (*to* DAVID). I forbid you to curse. Close your collar,

Amos. (*Of* AMOS *to* J.B.) Just ran two miles. (*He buttons another button on* AMOS, *indicating Amos's ball.*) How do you like the new method?

AMOS (*holds up ball*). Squeezin' a rubber ball.

J.B. What's that, for his fingers, heh?

DAVID *examines his arm.*

PAT. Fingers! That's the old forearm. A pitcher can have everything, but without a forearm? – Zero!

SHORY (*to* PAT, *of* DAVE). Are you going to settle this or is he going to get himself murdered in that house?

PAT. Who? What house? (*Recalling.*) Oh yes, Dave . . .

SHORY (*to* J.B.). Oh yes, Dave! (*To* PAT.) You're his father, For G . . . !

DAVID. All right. I got enough advice. Hester's coming here right away and we're going over to the house and we'll talk it out, and if . . .

SHORY. His brains are busted, how are you going to talk to him? He doesn't like you, he doesn't want you, he said he'd shoot you if you came onto his place. Now will you start from there and figure it out or you going to put it together in the hospital? (*Pause.*)

DAVID. What am I supposed to do then? Let him send her to that normal school? I might never see her again. I know how these things work.

SHORY. You don't know how these things work. Two years I waited in there for a boy to ask for the job I put up in the window. I could've made a big stink about it. I was a veteran, people ought to explain to the kids why I looked like this. But I learned something across the sea. Never go lookin' for trouble. I waited. And you came. Wait, Davey.

PAT. I'm inclined to agree with him, David.

DAVID. I've been waiting to marry Hester since we were babies. (*Sits on a barrel.*) God! How do you know when to wait and when to take things in your hand and make them happen?

SHORY. You can't make anything happen any more than a jellyfish makes the tides, David.

DAVID. What do you say, John?

J.B. I'd hate to see you battle old man Falk, but personally, Dave, I don't believe in waiting too long. A man's got to have faith, I think, and push right out into the current, and . . .

PAT (*leans forward, pointing*). Faith, David, is a great thing. Take me for instance. When I came back from the sea . . .

DAVID. What time you got, John . . . excuse me, Dad.

J.B. Twenty to eight.

DAVID (*to* SHORY). You giving me that shirt or must I push you off that chair?

PAT (*continuing*). I am speaking, David. When I came back from the sea . . .

SHORY (*pointing at* AMOS). Before you come back from the sea, you're going to kill him, running his ass off in the snow.

PAT. Kill him! Why it's common knowledge that pacing is indispensable for the arches. After all, a pitcher can have everything, but if his arches are not perfect . . . ?

SHORY. Zero!

PAT. Before I forget, do you know if that alcohol can be used for rubbing? (*Indicates the drum.*)

DAVID. There's only a couple of drops left.

AMOS. You sold it all today? (*Joyously to* PAT.) I told you he'd sell it all!

SHORY. Don't go making a genius out of your brother. Salesman hooked him. He bought alcohol in April when the sun was shining hot as hell.

AMOS. Yeah, but look how it froze up today!

SHORY. *He* didn't know it was going to freeze.

J.B. Maybe he did know. (*To* DAVE.) Did you, Dave?

DAVID (*stares into his memory*). Well, I . . . I kinda

thought . . .

PAT (*breaking in*). Speaking of geniuses, most people didn't know that there are two kinds; physical and mental. Take pitchers like Christy Matthewson now. Or Walter Johnson. There you have it in a nutshell. Am I right, J.B.?

SHORY. What've you got in a nutshell?

PAT (*the beginnings of confusion, his desire to protect* AMOS *and himself against everyone, tremble in him*). Just what I said. People simply refuse to concentrate. They don't know what they're supposed to be doing in their lives.

SHORY (*pointing to* DAVID). Example number one.

PAT (*rises to a self-induced froth of a climax*). I always left David to concentrate for himself. But take Amos then. When I got back from the sea I came home and what do I find? An infant in his mother's arms. I felt his body and I saw it was strong. And I said to myself, this boy is not going to waste out his life being seventeen different kind of things and ending up nothing. He's going to play baseball. And by ginger he's been throwin' against the target down the cellar seven days a week for twelve solid years! That's concentration! That's faith! That's taking your life in your own hands and moulding it to fit the thing you want. That's bound to have an effect . . . and don't you think they don't know it!

SHORY. Who knows it?

PAT (*with a cry*). I don't like everybody's attitude! (*Silence an instant.* ALL *staring at him.*) It's still winter! Can he play in the winter?

SHORY. Who are you talking about?

DAVID (*going away – towards the right – bored and disgusted*). Dad, he didn't say . . .

PAT. He doesn't have to say it. You people seem to think he's going to go through life pitching Sundays in the sand lots. (*To* ALL.) Pitching's his business; it's a regular business like . . . like running a store, or being a mechanic or anything else. And it happens that in the winter there is nothing to do in his business but sit home and wait!

J.B. Well, yeh, Pat, that's just what he ought to be doing.

PAT. Then why does everybody look at him as though . . . ?

He raises his hand to his head, utterly confused and ashamed for his outburst. A long pause like this.

DAVID (*unable to bear it, he goes to* PAT). Sit down, Dad. Sit down. (*He gets a barrel under* PAT, *who sits, staring, exhausted.*)

PAT. I can't understand it. Every paper in the county calls him a phenomenon.

As he speaks, DAVID, *feeling* PAT's *pain, goes right a few yards and stands looking away.*

Undefeated. He's ready for the big leagues. Been ready for three years. Who can explain a thing like that? Why don't they send a scout?

DAVID. I been thinking about that, Dad. Maybe you ought to call the Detroit Tigers again.

AMOS (*peevishly. This has been in him a long time*). He never called them in the first place.

PAT. Now, Amos . . .

DAVID (*reprimanding*). Dad . . .

AMOS. He didn't. He didn't call them. (*To* PAT.) I want him to know!

DAVID (*to* PAT). But last summer you said . . .

PAT. I've picked up the phone a lot of times . . . but I . . . I wanted it to happen . . . naturally. It ought to happen naturally, Dave.

SHORY. You mean you don't want to hear them say no.

PAT. Well . . . yes, I admit that. (*To* DAVID.) If I call now and demand an answer, maybe they'll have to say no. I don't want to put that word in their head in relation to Amos. It's a great psychological thing there. Once they refuse it's twice as hard to get them to accept.

DAVID. But, Dad, maybe . . . maybe they forgot to send a scout. Maybe they even thought they'd sent one and didn't, and when you call they'll thank you for reminding them. (*To* ALL.) I mean . . . can you *just wait for something to happen?*

SHORY (*claps*). Pinochle? Let's go. Come on, John! Pat!

They start for the store door.

J.B. (*glancing at his watch*). My wife'll murder me.

SHORY. Why? Pinochle leaves no odour on the breath.

PAT (*turning at ramp*). I want you to watch us, Amos. Pinochle is very good for the figuring sense. Help you on base play. Open your coat.

PAT *follows* SHORY *and* J.B. *into store.* AMOS *dutifully starts to follow, hesitates at the door, then closes it behind them and comes to* DAVID.

AMOS. Dave, I want to ask you something. (*He glances towards the door, then quietly.*) Take me over, will ya? (DAVE *just looks at him.*) Do something for me. I'm standing still. I'm not going anywhere. I swear I'm gettin' ashamed.

DAVID. Ah, don't, don't Ame.

AMOS. No, I am. Since I started to play everybody's been saying, (*Mimics.*) 'Amos is goin' some place, Amos is goin' someplace.' I been out of high school five years and I'm still taking spending money. I want to find a girl. I want to get married. I want to start doing things. You're movin' like a daisy cutter, Dave, you know how to *do*. Take me over.

DAVID. But I don't know half what Pop knows about baseball . . . about training or . . .

AMOS. I don't care, you didn't know anything about cars either, and look what you made here.

DAVID. What'd I make? I got nothin'. I still don't know

anything about cars.

AMOS. But you do. Everybody knows you know . . .

DAVID. Everybody's crazy. Don't envy me, Ame. If every car I ever fixed came rolling in here tomorrow morning and the guys said I did it wrong I wouldn't be surprised. I started on Shory's Ford and I got another one and another, and before I knew what was happening they called me a mechanic. But I ain't a trained man. You are. You *got* something . . . (*Takes his arm, with deepest feeling.*) and you're going to be great. Because you deserve it. You know something perfect. Don't look to me, I could be out on that street tomorrow morning, and then I wouldn't look so smart . . . Don't laugh at Pop. You're his whole life, Ame. You hear me? You stay with him.

AMOS. Gee Dave . . . you always make me feel so good. (*Suddenly like* PAT, *ecstatic.*) When I'm in the Leagues I'm gonna buy you . . . a . . . a whole goddam garage!

Enter HESTER *from the right. She is a full grown girl, a heartily developed girl. She can run fast, swim hard, and lift heavy things – not stylishly – but with the most economic and direct way to run, swim and lift. She has a loud, throaty laugh. Her femininity dwells in one fact – she loves* DAVID *with all her might, always has, and she doesn't feel she's doing anything when he's not around. The pallor of tragedy is nowhere near her. She enters breathless, not from running but from expectation.*

HESTER. David, he's home. (*Goes to* DAVID *and cups his face in her hands.*) He just came back! You ready? (*Looks around* DAVID's *shoulder at* AMOS.) Hullo, Ame, how's the arm?

AMOS. Good as ever.

HESTER. You do that long division I gave you?

AMOS. Well, I been working at it.

HESTER. There's nothing better'n arithmetic to sharpen you

up. You'll see, when you get on the diamond again, you'll
be quicker on base play. We better go, David.

AMOS (*awkwardly*). Well . . . good luck to ya. (*He goes to
the store door.*)

DAVID. Thanks, Ame.

AMOS *waves, goes through the door and closes it behind him.*

HESTER. What're you looking so pruney about? Don't you
want to go?

DAVID. I'm scared, Hess. I don't mind tellin' you. I'm
scared.

HESTER. Of a beatin'?

DAVID. You know I was never scared of a beatin'.

HESTER. We always knew we'd have to tell him, didn't we?

DAVID. Yeh, but I always thought that by the time we had
to, I'd be somebody. You know . . .

HESTER. But you are somebody . . .

DAVID. But just think of it from his side. He's a big farmer,
a hundred and ten of the best acres in the county.
Supposing he asks me – I only got three hundred and
ninety-four dollars, counting today . . .

HESTER. But we always said, when you had three fifty we'd
ask him.

DAVID. God, if I was a lawyer, or a doctor, or even a book-
keeper . . .

HESTER. A mechanic's good as a book-keeper!

DAVID. Yeh . . . but I don't know if I am a mechanic.
(*Takes her hand.*) Hess, listen, in a year maybe I could
build up some kind of a real business, something he could
look at and see.

HESTER. A year! Davey, don't . . . don't you . . . ?

DAVID. I mean . . . let's get married now, without asking
him.

HESTER. I told you, I can't . . .

DAVID. If we went away . . . far, far away . . .

HESTER. Wherever we went, I'd always be afraid he'd

knock on the door. You don't know what he can do when he's mad. He roared my mother to her grave . . . We have to face him with it, Davey. It seems now that I've known it since we were babies. When I used to talk to you at night through the kitchen window, when I'd meet you to ride around the quarry in Shory's car; even as far back as *The Last of the Mohicans* in 6B. I always knew we'd have to sit in the house together and listen to him roaring at us. We have to, Davey. (*She steps away, as though to give him a choice.*)

DAVID (*he smiles, a laugh escapes him*). You know, Hess, I don't only love you. You're my best friend.

HESTER *springs at him and kisses him. They are locked in the embrace when a figure enters from the right. It is* DAN DIBBLE, *a little sun-dried farmer, stolidly dressed – a mackinaw, felt hat. He hesitates a moment, then . . .*

DIBBLE. Excuse me . . . J.B. Feller . . . is J.B. Feller in here?

DAVID. J.B.? Sure. (*Points at back door.*) Go through there . . . he's in the store.

DIBBLE. Much obliged.

DAVID. That's all right, sir.

DIBBLE *tips his hat slightly to* HESTER, *goes a few yards towards the door, turns.*

DIBBLE. You . . . you Dave Beeves? Mechanic?

DAVID. Yes, sir, that's me.

DIBBLE *nods, turns, goes up the ramp and into the store, closing door behind him.* DAVID *looks after him.*

HESTER. Come, Davey.

DAVID. Yeh. I'll get my coat. (*He goes to rail at back where it hangs, starts to put it on.*) Gosh, I better change my shirt. Shory grabbed my clean one before. I guess he took it into the store with him.

HESTER (*knowingly*). He doesn't think you ought to go.

DAVID. Well . . . he was just kiddin' around. I'll only be a
minute.

DAVE *starts for the store door when it opens and J.B. surges
out full of excitement.* DIBBLE *follows him, then* AMOS, *then*
PAT, *and finally* SHORY *who looks on from his wheelchair
above the ramp.*

J.B. Hey, Dave! Dave, come here. (*To* DAN.) You won't
regret it, Dan . . . Dave . . . want you to meet my
brother-in-law from up in Burley. Dan Dibble.

DAVID. Yes, sir, how de do.

J.B. Dan's got a brand new Marmon . . . he's down here for
a funeral, see, and he's staying at my house . . .

DAVID (*to* J.B. *A note of faltering*). Marmon, did you say?

J.B. Yeh, Marmon. (*Imperatively.*) You know the Marmon,
Dave.

DAVID. Sure, ya . . . (*To* DAN.) Well, bring it around. I'll
be glad to work on her. I've got to go right now . . .

J.B. Dan, will you wait in my car? Just want to explain a
few things, I'll be right out and we'll go.

DIBBLE. Hurry up. It's cold out there. I'd like him to get it
fixed up by tomorrow. It's shakin' me up so, I think I'm
gettin' my appendix back.

J.B. (*jollying him to the door*). I don't think they grow back
once they're cut out . . .

DIBBLE. Well it feels like it. Be damned if I'll ever buy a
Marmon again. (DIBBLE *goes out.*)

J.B. (*he comes back to* DAVE). This idiot is one of the richest
farmers in the Burley district . . . He's got that mink
ranch I was tellin' you about.

DAVID. Say, I don't know anything about a Marmon . . .

J.B. Neither does he. He's got two vacuum cleaners in his
house and never uses nothin' but a broom. Now listen.
He claims she ain't hittin' right. I been tryin' the past two
weeks to get him to bring her down here to you. Now get

this. Besides the mink ranch he's got a wheat farm with five tractors.

HESTER. Five tractors!

J.B. He's an idiot, but he's made a fortune out of mink. Now you clean up this Marmon for him and you'll open your door to the biggest tractor farms in the state. There's big money in tractor work, you know that. He's got a thousand friends and they follow him. They'll follow him here.

DAVID. Uh, huh. But I don't know anything about tractors.

HESTER. Oh, heck, you'll learn!

DAVID. Yeah, but I can't learn on his tractors.

HESTER. Yeah, but . . .

J.B. Listen! This could be the biggest thing that ever happened to you. The Marmon's over at my house. He's afraid to drive her any further on the snow. I'll bring her over and you'll go to work. All right?

DAVID. Yeah, but look, John, I . . .

J.B. You better get in early and start on her first thing in the morning. All right?

HESTER (*with a loud bubble of laughter*). David, that's wonderful!

DAVID (*quickly*). See, if we waited, Hess. In six months, maybe less, I'd have something to show!

HESTER. But I'm going to Normal in a week if we don't do it now!

SHORY. You're pushing him, Hester.

HESTER (*a sudden outburst at* SHORY). Stop talking to him! A person isn't a frog, to wait and wait for something to happen!

SHORY. He'll fight your father if you drag him there tonight! And your father can kill him!

DAVID (*takes her hand. Evenly*). Come on, Hess. We'll go. (*To* J.B.) Bring the car over, I'll be back later . . .

But J.B. *is staring off right, down the driveway.* DAVE *turns, with* HESTER *and all to follow his stare. She steps a foot away from him. Enter* ANDREW FALK, *a tall, old man, hard as iron, near-sighted, slightly stooped. Sound of idling motor outside.*

J.B. (*after a moment*). I'll bring the car, Dave. Five minutes.

DAVID (*affecting a business-like, careless flair*). Right J.B., I'll fix him up. (*As* J.B. *goes out.*) And thanks loads, John!

FALK *has been looking at* HESTER, *who dares every other moment to look up from the floor at him.* DAVID *turns to* FALK, *desperately controlling his voice.* PAT *enters from* SHORY's *store.*

Evening, Mr Falk. You want to go in to Shory's store? There's chairs there . . . (FALK *turns deliberately, heavily looks at him.*) You left your engine running. Stay awhile. Let me shut it off.

FALK. You willin' to push it?

DAVID. Oh, battery run down?

FALK (*caustically*). I don't know what else would prevent her from turnin' over without a push. (*To* HESTER.) I'll see you home.

HESTER (*smiling, she goes to him, but does not touch him*). We were just comin' to the house, Daddy.

FALK. Go on home, Hester.

DAVID. We'd like to talk to you, Mr Falk. (*Indicating the store.*) We could all go . . .

FALK (*in reply*). Go on home, Hester.

DAVID (*with a swipe at indignation*). I'd like for her to be here, Mr Falk . . .

FALK (*he does not even look at David*). I'll be home right away. (*He takes her arm and moves her to the right. She digs her heels in.*)

HESTER (*a cry*). Daddy, why . . . !

She breaks off, looking into his face. With a sob she breaks from him and runs off right. He turns slowly to DAVID, *takes a breath.*

DAVID (*angering*). That ain't gonna work any more, Mr Falk. We're old enough now.

PAT (*reasonably*). Look, Falk, why don't we . . . ?

FALK (*to* DAVID, *without so much as a glance at* PAT). This is the last time I'm ever goin' to talk to you, Beeves. You . . .

DAVID. Why is it you're the only man who hates me like this? Everybody else . . .

FALK. Nobody but me knows what you are.

SHORY (*from the store doorway*). What is he? What are you blowin' off about?

FALK (*his first rise of voice. He points at* SHORY). The good God gave you your answer long ago! Keep your black tongue in your head when I'm here.

SHORY (*nervously. To* DAVID). His brains are swimmin', don't you see? What are you botherin' with him for . . . !

FALK (*roaring, he takes a stride towards* SHORY). Shut up, you . . . you whoremonger! You ruined your last woman on *this* earth! The good God saw to that.

SHORY (*with a screech of fury*). You don't scare me, Falk. You been dead twenty years, why don't you bury yourself?

FALK *strangely relaxes, walks away from* SHORY's *direction, raising his shoulder to run his chin on his coat collar. The motor outside stalls. His head cocks towards right.*

DAVID (*pointing to the right*). Your car stalled. I'll start her up for you.

FALK. Don't touch anything I own! (*Pause.*) What were you doin' that night I caught you with her by the river? You got backbone enough to tell me that?

DAVID (*recalls*). Oh . . . we were kids then . . . just talkin', that's all.

FALK. You never come and ask me if she could talk to you.

You come sneakin' every time, like a rat through the fences.

DAVID. Well . . . Hess was always scared to ask you, and I . . . I guess I got it from her.

FALK. You're scared of me now too, and you know why, Beeves? Nobody but me knows what you are.

DAVID. Why, what am I?

FALK. You're a lost soul, a lost man. You don't know the nights I've watched you, sittin' on the river ice, fishin' through a hole – alone, alone like an old man with a boy's face. Or makin' you a fire in Keldon's woods where nobody could see. And that Sunday night you nearly burned down the church . . .

DAVID. I was nowhere near the church that night . . . !

FALK. It couldn't have been nobody else! When the church burned there never was a sign from God that was so clear.

AMOS. He was down the cellar with me when the church burned.

FALK (*looks at* AMOS). I am not blind. (*Turns back to* DAVID.) The man Hester marries is gonna know what he's about. He's gonna be a steady man that I can trust with what I brought forth in this world. He's gonna know his God, he's gonna know where he came from and where he's goin'. You ain't that man. (*He turns to go.*)

DAVID. I'm marryin' Hester, Mr Falk. (FALK *stops, turns.*) I'm sorry, but we're going to marry.

FALK. Beeves, if you ever step onto my land again, I'll put a bullet through you, may God write my words . . . I don't fool, Beeves. Don't go near her again. (*Points to* SHORY.) No man who could find a friend in that lump of corruption is going to live in my daughter's house. (*He starts to go again.*)

DAVID. I'm marryin' Hester, Mr Falk! We're gonna do it!

FALK. You'll sleep with your shroud first, Beeves. I'm old enough to know what I'll do. Stay away!

He goes to the right edge of the stage, and hesistates, looking off right in the direction of his stalled car. DAVID *starts doubtfully toward him, looking over his shoulder.*

SHORY (*rolling down the ramp*). Let him start it himself! Don't be a damned fool!

FALK *hurries out.*

PAT (*pointing right*). Maybe you ought to give him a push.

SHORY. Not on your life! (*He pushes himself between* DAVE *and the door.*) Get away from there, go on!

DAVID (*looking off right all the time*). Shory . . . he's going . . . what can I say to him . . . (*Starts to go right.*) I'll help him.

SHORY (*pushes him back*). Get away! (*Calling off right.*) That's it, Grandpa, push it . . . push it! Harder, you crazy bastard, it's only half a mile! Go ahead, harder! (*Laughs wildly, mockingly.*)

DAVID (*wrenches the chair around*). Stop it!

SHORY. You can't talk to that man! You're through, you damned fool.

DAVID (*suddenly*). Come on, Ame, we'll pick up Hester on the road before he gets home. I'm going to do it tonight, by God . . .

AMOS (*in ecstasy at the thought of action, he wings the ball across the stage*). Let's go!

PAT (*grabs* DAVE). No, Dave . . .

DAVE (*furiously*). No, I gotta do it, Dad!

PAT. I forbid it (*To* AMOS.) I forbid you to go. (*To* DAVID.) She's his daughter and he's got a right, David.

DAVID. What right has he got! *She* wants me!

PAT. Then let her break from him. That's not your province.

DAVID. She's scared to death of him! The whole thing is between me and Hester. *I don't understand why I can't have that girl!*

SHORY (*sardonically*). Must there be a reason?

DAVID (*he stops for an instant as though a light flashed on him*). Yes, there has to be a reason! I did everything a man could do. *I didn't do anything wrong and* . . .

SHORY. You didn't have to! (DAVE *stares at* SHORY.) A man is a jellyfish. The tide goes in and the tide goes out. About what happens to him, a man has very little to say. When are you going to get used to it?

DAVID stands staring.

PAT. You better go home and sleep, Dave. Sleep is a great doctor, you know.

SHORY (*gently*). He said it, Dave.

Enter J.B. in a hurry.

J.B. Where is Dan? Where's the Marmon?

PAT. He didn't come here.

J.B. That ox! I tell him I'll drive it over for him. No, Dan Dibble don't allow anybody behind the wheel but himself. I go into the house to tell Ellie I'm goin' and when I come out he's gone. (*Starts to go right.*) That seven passenger moron . . .

DAVID. He probably decided to go back home to Burley.

J.B. No, I'm sure he's tryin' to get here. Rugged individualist! I'll find him on some dirt road some place . . . (*He shuts up abruptly as a door slams outside.*)

All look right.

DAVID (*alarmed*). Hester!

He quickly goes off right. For an instant AMOS, PAT, and SHORY are galvanised. AMOS goes off and returns immediately supporting DAN DIBBLE who is shaking all over and seems about to collapse in distress.

DIBBLE (*on entering*). God help me, God in Heaven help me . . .

Enter DAVID *and* J.B. *helping* HESTER. *She is sobbing on* DAVID'*s arm and he is trying to lift her face up.*

DAVID. Stop crying, what's the matter? Hester, stop it, what happened? J.B.!

DIBBLE (*goes prayerfully to* HESTER). I couldn't see him, Miss, how in the world could I see him? His car had no lights . . .

HESTER'*s loud sob cuts him off.*

DAVID (*to* DAN). What happened? What did you do?

DIBBLE. Oh, God in Heaven, help me . . .

J.B. (*goes to him, pulls his hands down*). Dan . . . stop that . . . For Pete's sake, what happened?

DIBBLE. This girl's father . . . an old man . . . I couldn't see him . . . He was pushing a car without lights. There were no lights at all, and he walked out from behind just as I came on him.

But for HESTER'*s subsiding sobs, there is silence for a moment. She looks at* DAVID, *who looks once at her, then comes to life.*

DAVID (*to* DAN). Where is he now?

DIBBLE (*points upstage*). I took him to his house . . . she was there. It happened a few feet from his house.

DAVID (*horrified*). Well, why didn't you get a doctor! (*He starts for the back door.*)

HESTER. No . . . he's dead, Davey.

Almost at the ramp, DAVID *stops as though shot. After an instant he turns quickly. He comes as in a dream a few yards towards her, and, as in a dream, halts, staring at her.*

He's dead.

DAVID *stares at her. Then turns his head to* PAT, AMOS, SHORY, DAN . . . *as though to seek reality. Then looking at her once more he goes to the nail barrel and sits.*

DAVID (*whisper*). I'll be darned. (*Goes to* HESTER . . . *after a moment.*) I'm so sorry.

HESTER. It was nobody's fault. Oh that poor man!

PAT (*goes to* DAVID). You better . . . come home, David.

DAVID (*he gets up, goes to* HESTER, *takes her hand*). Hess? I really am sorry.

HESTER *looks at him, a smile comes to her face. She thankfully throws her arms around him and sobs.*

Don't Hess . . . don't cry anymore. Please Hess . . . John, take her to your house for tonight, heh?

J.B. I was going to do that. (*Takes* HESTER'*s arm.*) Come on, baby. I'll tend to everything.

DAVID. Goodnight, Hess. You sleep, heh?

HESTER. You mustn't feel any fault, Davey.

DAVID. I could have gotten him started, that's all. He said . . . (*A filament of sardonic laughter.*) . . . don't touch anything I own.

HESTER. It wasn't your fault! You understand? In any way.

DAVID (*nods inconclusively*). Go to bed, go ahead.

J.B. (*leading* HESTER *off*). We'll get you home, and you'll sleep.

DIBBLE (DAN *follows them until he gets to the right edge. Turning to* DAVID). If there's any blood on the car will you clean it off? Please, will you?

DAN *goes,* DAVID *looks after them.*

SHORY. Get me home, will you, Dave?

DAVID. Huh? No, I'll stay awhile. I want to look at the car. You take him, will you, Dad?

PAT (*taking hold of the back of* SHORY'*s chair*). Sure. Come on, Amos.

SHORY. Well, wake up, jellyfish. A hundred and ten of the best acres in the valley. Not bad, eh?

DAVID (*stunned*). Just like that.

SHORY. Never happens any other way, brother. (*Almost intones it.*) Jellyfish don't swim . . . It's the tide moves him . . . out and in . . . out and in . . . and in. Keep it in mind. (To PAT.) Let's go, father.

They push him out as DAVE stands there lost in a dream.

Curtain.

Scene Two

The barn near dawn.

DAVID *is lying under the front end of the Marmon. Beside it the hood stands on end on the floor.* DAVID *is lying under the engine with one light near his head, hurriedly tightening a nut on the pan. There is one other light on, over the bench, but this is shaded. After a moment,* DAVID *hurriedly slides out from under and eagerly looking at the engine, wipes his hands. He is about to get into the car to start it when a soft knock from offstage right is heard. Startled he peers through the darkness.*

DAVID. Who's that? (*Surprised.*) Hester . . .

HESTER (*she comes out of the darkness at right*). Aren't you finished yet?

DAVID (*glancing defensively at the car*). What are you doing up? What time is it?

HESTER. It's almost five. I called your house, I just couldn't sleep. Belle said you were still here. Can I watch you?

DAVID. . . It's pretty cold in here, you'll catch cold.

HESTER (*she goes to him, takes his face in her hands, and kisses him*). You didn't kiss me yet.

DAVID (*with growing ill-ease*). Please, Hess, I gotta figure something out here. I wish . . . I wish you'd leave me alone for a while. Please.

HESTER (*with quiet astonishment – and compassion*). Haven't you figured it out yet?

DAVID. Oh, I got it just about, but not . . . (*Stops.*) Hess, please leave me alone.

DAVID *walks from her and pretends to study the engine.*

HESTER. Davey.

DAVID. Ya?

HESTER. You're *going* to be able to fix it, aren't you?

DAVID. Don't you think I can?

HESTER. I know you can.

DAVID. Then why do you ask me?

HESTER. Because . . . in the Burley garage they didn't know how to fix it.

DAVID (*he straightens. Slight pause*). How do you know?

HESTER. J.B. told me. He's going to tell you in the morning after you're finished. He didn't want to scare you about it.

DAVID (*with growing fear*). That can't be. They got regular trained mechanics in the Burley garage.

HESTER. But it's true. Mr Dibble said they wanted to take the whole thing apart and charge him a hundred and fifty dollars, and he wouldn't let them because . . .

DAVID (*comes to her anxiously*). Why'd they want to take the whole thing apart?

HESTER (*seeing his bewilderment clearer*). Well, I don't know, Davey . . .

DAVID. Well what'd they tell him was wrong? Don't you remember . . . ?

HESTER (*her sob threatening*). Well, Davey, don't shout at me that way, I don't know anything about cars . . . (*She begins to cry.*)

DAVID (*with the pain of guilt*). Oh, Hester, don't cry, please. I'll fix it, I'll find out what the matter is, please, stop it, will you?

The pain it causes him makes him turn and almost march to the car. On the point of weeping himself.

I never *heard* an engine make that sound. I took the pan off, I took the head off, I looked at the valves; I just don't know what it is, Hess! It's turning off centre somewhere and I can't find it, I can't!

HESTER (*her sobbing vanishes as she senses his loss*). That's all right, Davey, it'll be all right. Maybe you better go to bed. You look so tired . . . It really doesn't matter so much.

DAVID (*she growing taller upon his guilt*). Gosh, Hess . . . there never was a girl like you. (*He goes to her and kisses her.*) I swear there never was.

HESTER. Don't ever try for anything I want, if it worries you too much to get it, Davey.

DAVID (*he kisses her cheek. With swift resolution*). You go home and go to bed. I'll find out what's the matter. I'll do it! You go.

HESTER. All right, Davey, 'cause J.B. was telling Mr Dibble such great things about you . . . He's got a marvellous thing to tell you in the morning.

DAVID. What?

HESTER. I can't tell you till you finish . . .

DAVID. Please, Hess, what'd he say?

HESTER. No, fix it first. (*Pause.*) J.B. wants to tell you himself. He made me promise. Goodnight.

DAVID. Goodnight, Hess.

HESTER (*going and waving*). And don't worry . . . about anything, okay?

DAVID. . . . I won't.

He watches her go, then turns to the car, goes and stands over it, tapping his nose with his finger thoughtfully. Then lightly punching his fist into his palm in the heartbeat rhythm, faster, then faster . . . then . . . Bursting out in loud whisper.

God damn!

The sound of a man walking into the shop rather slowly from offstage right is heard. DAVE *turns toward the sound and stands still watching.* GUSTAV EBERSON *enters. He is a strong man, his suit is pressed but too small for him. He wears a white shirt. A plain brown overcoat. He is smiling warmly, but with the self-effacing manner of an intruder.* DAVID *says nothing as he approaches.*

GUS (*a slight German accent*). Excuse me, are you Mr Beeves?

DAVID. Yeh. (*Slight pause.*)

GUS. My name is Eberson . . . Gus Eberson . . . (*With an apologetic nod and smile.*) Are you very busy? I could of course come back. Four o'clock in the morning is not the best time to visit.

DAVID. I'm, busy . . . but what can I do for you?

GUS. I moved into town last night. And I couldn't wait to see my first morning. I noticed your light. I thought we ought to know each other.

DAVID (*taken*). I'm glad to know you. I was almost hoping you were a hold-up man and you'd knock me unconscious.

GUS. I didn't mean to walk in so invisibly; I am opening a repair garage on the other end of the avenue.

DAVID. Repair garage? You mean to repair cars?

GUS (*earnestly, worriedly*). I want to assure you, Mr Beeves, that if I didn't think there is plenty of business here for both of us I would never set up a place in this town.

DAVID (*a faint tightness cramps his voice*). Oh, there's plenty of business for two here. Plenty! Where is your shop?

GUS. Over there on Poplar Street, right next to the grocery store.

DAVID. Oh, that place. Gosh, nobody's been in that building for years. We used to say it was haunted.

GUS. Maybe it is! (*Laughs lightly at himself*). I have very little machinery. As a matter of fact . . . (*Quite happily.*) . . .

I have very little money too. So possibly I will not be troubling you very long.

DAVID (*with emphatic assurance*). Oh, you'll make out all right. (*Vaguely indicates the shop.*) There's nothin' to it. You come from around here?

GUS. No, I was with the Fords Company, the River Rouge plant for several years. This last year and four months I was by the Hudson Motor people.

DAVID (*breathlessly*). Well . . . I guess you oughta know your stuff.

GUS (*sensing . . . extra hearty, therefore*). What is there to know? You are probably much better than I am!

DAVID. No, that's all right, I just meant . . .

GUS. I am not in the world to become rich. I was doing very well in Detroit.

DAVID. Then why'd you come here?

GUS. It is my nature. I cannot get used, I shall run, run, run, I shall work, work, work, all the time rushing. To tell you the truth, I was five years with Fords and not one good friend did I have. Here, I hope, it will be more conducive to such activities as I always enjoy. A small town and so forth. I am Austrian, you understand. . . . Meanwhile I hope you will not object too strongly of my arrival?

DAVID (*entranced*). Hell no. Lots of luck to you! I got no right to object. (*Extends his hand jerkily.*)

GUS (*shakes hands*). Rights is not the question. I want to be welcome. Otherwise I will . . .

DAVID (*softly;* GUS *holds onto his hand*). No. . . . You're welcome here . . . You are.

GUS. Thank you . . . Thank you.

Laughs softly, thankfully. Their hands part. GUS *turns a slow full circle looking at the shop.* DAVID *watches him like a vision. At last the Austrian faces him again. Quietly.*
How old are you?

DAVID. Goin' on twenty-two.

GUS (*indicating the car, the shop . . . everything*). How . . . how did you know what to do? You studied somewhere mechanics?

DAVID (*with pride and yet uneasiness. The Austrian has grown very tall in his eyes*). Oh no – I just picked it up kinda. (*Wanders near the Marmon as though to hide it.*) But I guess I got plenty to learn.

GUS. No, no! The best mechanics is made in this fashion. You must not feel at all . . . how shall I say . . . at a loss.

Pause. They hold each other's gaze in a moment of understanding. Slowly the Austrian's eyes turn toward the Marmon. DAVID, *as though relinquishing it, moves aside now, not screening it any longer.*

What's his trouble?

DAVID (*still entranced, and yet he must laugh as he confesses*). You got me there. I've been at it all night . . .

GUS (*sauntering easily to the car*). Oh? What he complains of?

DAVID (*for a moment he holds back; then the last shred of resentment fades and he bursts out*). She runs with a peculiar kind of a shudder . . . like a rubbing somewhere inside.

GUS. She misfires?

DAVID. That's what's so funny. She fires on eight and the carburettor's set right on the button.

Pause. GUS *looks down at the engine.* DAVID *is bent over watching his face.*

GUS. If you . . . feel like it, you can start the engine.

DAVID (*looks at him in silence*). You . . . you know what it is?

GUS (*reaches to him quickly*). Look, boy, tell me and I will leave the town, I'll never come back.

DAVID. No, no . . . I want it to be . . . just the way it ought to be, the way it . . . happened.

DAVID *goes to car door, gets in – starts the motor. The*

Austrian stands listening for five seconds, then snaps his hand for the motor to be switched off. It is quiet again. DAVID *comes slowly out of the car and stands beside the Austrian, watching him.*

GUS. It is very rare. In a car so new. It comes sometimes with the Marmon, however.

DAVID (*softly*). What is it?

GUS (*turns straight to him*). The crankshaft is sprung.

DAVID (*for a long moment he stares into the Austrian's face*). How could you tell by listening?

GUS. Same way you do for pistons. You know. You going to work now?

DAVID (*looks at the car*). Ya.

He hurries around the front of the car, picks up a wrench, comes around and sets the wrench on a heat nut and starts forcing it.

GUS (*hesitates for a moment, then lays his hand on* DAVID). Don't take the head off. (DAVID *stops.*) I mean . . . you don't need to, necessarily. (DAVID *stops moving. The wrench clatters out of his hand. He stands nearly trembling before the Austrian, who suddenly turns.*) I'll go.

DAVID (*stops him*). No, I always knew a time would come when . . . this would happen. I mean somebody like you would come, and then I'd just . . . pack up. I knew it all the time . . .

GUS. That's nonsense. You fixed plenty cars no doubt; you're a mechanic . . .

DAVID. No, I'm not really. I don't know anything about metals and ratios and . . . I was almost going to tow it to the shop in Newton. Would you tell me what to do?

GUS. Gladly. And maybe sometimes I need a hand you'll drop by. All right?

DAVID. Oh I'd be glad to.

GUS (*grips his shoulder and points under the car*). First you take the pan down.

DAVID (*slight pause*). Ya?

GUS. Then you drop the bearings. Label them so you know where to put them back.

DAVID. Ya?

GUS. Then you drop the main bearings for the crankshaft.

DAVID. Ya?

GUS. Then you drop the shaft itself. Take it up to Newton, is a good shop there. Tell them to exchange for a new shaft.

DAVID. Can't I straighten this one?

GUS. Is not possible for you.

DAVID. Could you straighten it?

GUS. That would depend – but I sold my instruments for this. You go to work now. Go ahead.

DAVID (*starts to move*). You in a hurry to go away?

GUS. I'll stay, I'll watch you.

DAVID (*thankfully*). Okay. (*He gets down on his knees and is about to get under the car.*) You feel like workin'? Just for a couple of minutes?

GUS. You would like me to?

DAVID. I always wanted to see how somebody else works. Y'know?

GUS. All right, come on. We rip her open. (*He pulls off his coat.*) You got a socket, a quarter inch?

DAVID (*a new excitement in him*). I ain't got sockets yet, but . . .

GUS. That's all right, give me an open end. (DAVID *goes for the wrench quickly.*) How much oil you got in here?

DAVID (*finding the wrench*). Just a couple of quarts. I just ran her a minute. I'll drain her.

He gets under car quickly, opening the drain nuts, setting a can under it, as . . .

GUS. Are you married?

DAVID. Not yet . . . (*Under the car.*) but pretty soon . . . are you?

GUS (*ready to work, he kneels on one knee beside the car*). No, but I am always hopeful. There is a nice red-headed girl in this town? (*Preparing to slide under.*)

DAVID (*laughs*). She got to be red-headed?

GUS. Yes, I would prefer such a colour. It always seemed to me in a small American town would be many red-headed girls. Probably this is because in general I like a small town. When this car has to be ready? (*Slides under.*)

DAVID *moves to make room; sits on his heels beside the car.*

DAVID. Eleven in the morning, if possible. You think it can?

GUS. Oh, plenty of time. You got a car to take this shift to Newton?

DAVID. Yeh, that Ford outside. Oh – my back.

GUS. Spread out, take it easy.

DAVID (*relaxes on the floor*). Gosh, you sure swing that wrench. Lots of times I do something and I wonder how they'd do it in the factory – you know, officially.

GUS. In the factory also they wonder sometimes how it's done officially.

DAVID (*laughs*). Yeh, I bet. (*Pause.* GUS *works.*) Gosh, I suddenly feel awful tired. I been at it all night, y'know?

GUS. Sleep, go ahead. I'll wake you when it gets interesting.

DAVID. . . . Don't think you're doing this for nothing; I'll split the bill with you.

GUS. Nonsense. (*Laughs..*) We'll even it up sometime. One hand washes the other.

DAVID'S *head comes down on his arm, his face towards the Austrian. For several moments* GUS *works in silence.* DAVID'S *breathing comes in longer draughts.* GUS, *noticing his eyes closed . . .*

Mr Beeves?

DAVID *sleeps.*

GUS *comes out from under the car, gets his own coat and lays it over* DAVID *and looks down at him. A smile comes to his face, he shakes his head wondrously, and looks from* DAVID *all around the shop. Then, happily, and with a certain anticipation, he whispers . . .*

America!

He bends, slides under the car as the lights go down.

The lights come up on the same scene. From the large barn doors a wide shaft of sunlight is pouring in. DAVID *is asleep where he was before, the coat still on him. But now the car is off the jack, and the hood is in place over the engine. The tools are in a neat pile nearby.*

Enter J.B., DAN DIBBLE, HESTER, PAT *and* AMOS.

J.B. (*as they enter. To* DAN). We're a little early, so if he needs more time you'll wait, Dan. . . . (*Looks at* DAVID. *Quietly.*) What'd he do, sleep here all night?

AMOS. Must've. He never come home.

J.B. (*to* DAN). That's the type of character you're dealing with. I hope you don't forget to thank him.

DIBBLE (*fearfully touching the fender*). It looks just the same as when I brought it. You think it's fixed?

HESTER *goes to* DAVID.

J.B. (*looks at* DAVID). Don't worry, it's fixed.

HESTER. Should I wake him?

J.B. Go ahead. I want to tell him right away.

HESTER (*bends over and shakes him lightly*). Davey? Davey?

DAVID. Huh?

HESTER. Wake up. J.B.'s here. It's morning. (*Laughs.*) Look at him!

DAVID. Oh. (*Sits up and sees* J.B. *and* DIBBLE.) Oh ya, ya.

He gets up quickly catching the coat as it falls from him. He looks at the coat for an instant.

HESTER (*fixing his shirt straight*). Is it all done?

when you're young. Sleep anywhere. Nothin' bothers
you.

DAVID. What time is it?

J.B. About half past ten.

DAVID (*astonished and frightened*). Half past ten! Gosh, I
didn't mean to sleep that long . . . ! (*Looks around,
suddenly anxious.*)

HESTER (*laughs*). You look so *funny!*

J.B. Well, how'd you do, Dave, all finished?

DAVID. Finished? Well, uh . . . (*He looks at the car.*)

J.B. If you're not, Dan can wait.

DAVID. Ya . . . just a second, I . . . (*He looks around the
shop.*)

HESTER. Looking for your tools? They're right on the floor
here.

DAVID (*he keeps looking all around for an instant. Looks at the
tools*). Oh, okay. (*He looks at the car as though it were
explosive. He lifts the hood and looks at the engine as . . .*)

J.B. How was it, tough job?

DAVID. Heh? Ya, pretty tough.

J.B. Anything wrong . . . ?

DAVID. No, I . . . (*He gets on his knees and looks under the
engine.*)

DIBBLE. Can I start her up now?

DAVID (*gets to his feet, looks at everyone as though in a dream*).
Okay, try her. Wait a minute, let me.

DIBBLE (*following him to the car door*). Now don't dirty the
upholstery . . .

J.B. Don't worry about the upholstery, Dan, come over
here.

DIBBLE (*coming to the front of car where* J.B. *and* HESTER
are). They always get in with their dirty clothes . . .

The engine starts. It hums smoothly, quietly. J.B. *turns
proudly smiling to* DAN: *who creeps closer to it and listens.*
HESTER *watches* J.B., *teetering on the edge of expectation,*

then watches DAN. *After a moment the engine is shut off.*
DAVID *comes out of the car, comes slowly into view, his eyes*
wide.

PAT (*to* DAN, *of* DAVE). Highly skilled, highly skilled.

J.B. (*beaming, to* DIBBLE). Well, you damn fool?

DIBBLE (*excitedly*). Why she does, she does sound fine. (*He*
snoops around the car.)

DAVID. Look, J.B., I . . .

J.B. (*raises his fist and bangs on the fender*). Goddam, Dave,
I always said it! You know what you did?

HESTER. Davey, J.B.'s going to . . .

J.B. (*to* HESTER). I'm paying for it, at least let me tell it.
Dan, come over here first and tell Dave what they did to
you in Burley. Listen to this one, Dave. Pat, I want you
to hear this.

PAT *and* AMOS *come into the group.*

DIBBLE (*feeling the edge of the fender*). I think he bumped it
here.

J.B. Oh, the hell with that, come over here and tell him.
(DIBBLE *comes.*) What about that guy in Burley?

DIBBLE. Well, there's a garage in Burley does tractor work.
But he's not reasonable . . .

J.B. Tell him what he does.

DIBBLE. I brought this one to him and he says I'll have to
take her plumb apart, every screw and bolt of her. He
had his mind set on charging me a hundred and thirty-
one dollars for the job. So, I figured it was just about time
I stopped subsidizin' the Burley Garage Incorporated.

PAT. That's intelligent, Mr Dibble.

DAVID. Did he tell you what was wrong with the car? The
Burley man?

DIBBLE. Well, yes, he did, he always tells you something,
but I can't . . . Now wait a minute . . . These things have
a dingus they call a . . . a crankshaft? He said it was

crooked, or busted, or dented . . .

J.B. (*laughs – to* DAVID, *then back to* DAN). On a brand new Marmon! What the hell did he want with the crankshaft?

PAT. Scandalous.

DAVID. Look, J.B., lemme tell you . . .

J.B. (*drawing* DAVID *and* DAN *together*). Go ahead, David. And listen to this, Dan. This is the first honest word you ever heard out of a mechanic. (*To* DAVID.) Go on, tell this poor sucker what the matter was.

DAVID *stands dumbly, looking into* J.B.*'s ecstatic face. He turns to* HESTER.

HESTER (*hardly able to stand still. Pridefully*). Tell him, Davey!

DAVID (*turns back to* J.B. *He sighs*). Just a lot of small things, that's all.

DAVID *walks a few steps away to a fender and absently touches it. It could be taken for modesty.* AMOS *is now to the side, resting a foot on the car bumper – watching in wonder.*

J.B. Well? What do you say, Danny? Now you're looking at a *mechanic*!

PAT (*to* DAN, *of* DAVE). At the age of six he fixed the plug on an iron.

DIBBLE (*goes to* DAVID). Look, David. I have a proposition for you. Whenever there's a job to do on my tractors charge me for parts and that's all. If you'd do that for me, I could guarantee you more . . .

DAVID. I'm much obliged to you, Mr Dibble, but I'm not tooled up for tractor work . . .

J.B. Now wait a minute . . .

DAVID (*almost shouting with tension*). Let me say something will you? To work on heavy engines like that, and tractors in general a man has got to be a . . . well, I'm not tooled up for it, that's all, I haven't got the machinery.

J.B. (*businesslike*). But you've got the machinery.

HESTER. Listen to this, Davey!

DAVID *looks at him.*

J.B. You go out and buy everything you want. Fix up this building. Lay out a concrete driveway in the front. I'll pay the bills. Give me one per cent on my money. (*Roundly.*) Let me be some good in my life!

DAVID (*as though a fever were rising in him, his voice begins to soar*). I don't know if I'm ready for that, J.B. . . . I'd have to study about tractors . . . I . . .

J.B. Then study! Now's the *time*, Dave. You're young, strong . . . !

PAT (*to* DAN). He's very strong.

DIBBLE (*taking out a roll*). How much do I owe you, boy?

DAVID *looks at* DAN.

DAVID. Owe me?

J.B. Make it sixty dollars flat, Dave. Since it wasn't as hard as we thought. (DAVID *looks at* J.B. *who won't wait for him to object.*) Sixty flat, Dan.

DIBBLE (*counts laboriously, peeling off each bill into* DAVID's *unwilling hand*). One, two, three . . . (*Continues.*)

HESTER (*joyously amused at* DAN). What're those, all ones?!

DIBBLE. All I carry is ones. Never can tell when you'll leave a five by mistake. (*Continues counting.*) Government ought to print different sizes.

J.B. How's it feel to have two stars, heh, Pat? (*With a sweep of his hand.*) I can see a big red sign out there way up in the air. Dave Beeves, Incorporated, Tractor Station . . .

HESTER *has noticed the coat beside car.*

HESTER (*holding the coat up*). Did you get a new coat?

DIBBLE *continues counting into* DAVID's *hand.*

HESTER. Huh?

Quickly turns to HESTER *and the coat.* DAN DIBBLE *continues counting.* DAVID *stares at the coat, suddenly in the full blast of all the facts. Now all but* DIBBLE *are looking at the coat.*

AMOS (*feels the coat*). Where'd you get this?
DIBBLE. Hold still! Fifty-three, fifty-four, fifty . . .

DAVID *looks at* AMOS, *then down at his hand into which the money is still dropping. He then looks again at* AMOS . . . AMOS *to him.*

AMOS. What's the matter?
HESTER. What's come over you?

DAVID *suddenly hands the money to* HESTER.

DIBBLE. Say!
DAVID (*his hand recedes from the bills as though they were burning. To* HESTER). Take it, will ya? I . . .

He starts to point somewhere off right as though he were being called. Then his hand drops . . . and with gathering speed he strides out.

HESTER (*astonished*). Davey . . . (*She hurries to watch him leaving, to the right, halts.*) Why . . . he's running! (*Calling in alarm.*) Davey! (*She runs out.*)

J.B., PAT *and* DAN *stand, watching them open-mouthed as they disappear down the driveway.* AMOS *is centre, downstage.*

DIBBLE. What in the world come over the boy? I didn't finish payin' him.

They stand looking right. AMOS *looks at the coat. He starts turning it inside out, examining it carefully, perplexed . . .*

Slow Curtain.

ACT TWO

Scene One

June. Three years later. The living room of the FALK's – *now* DAVID's *house. A farmhouse room, but brightly done over. Solid door to outside at the right. In the back wall, right a swinging door to the dining room. A stairway at the back, its landing at the left. A door, leading to an office in the bedroom, down left. One window at left. Two windows flanking the door to outside at right. Good blue rug, odd pieces, some new, some old. Oak. A pair of well-used rubber boots beside the door.*

The stage is empty. A perfect summer day, not too hot. Noon. After a moment the doorbell rings.

HESTER (*from above, shouts excitedly*). They're here! Davey!

DAVID (*hurrying down the stairs, buttoning on a white shirt. He wears pressed pants, shined shoes, his hair has just been combed; shouting up*). I'll get it, I'm going!

HESTER (*her head sticking out at the junction of banister and ceiling. She quickly surveys the room as* DAVID *comes off the stairs*). Get your boots out of there! I just fixed up the house!

The bell rings.

DAVID (*calling towards the door*). Just a minute! (*getting the boots together. To* HESTER.) Go on, get dressed, it's almost noon! (*He opens door to dining room.*)

HESTER. Don't put them in there! They're filthy! Down the cellar!

DAVID. But I always put them in here!

HESTER. But you promised once the house is painted!

Door opens. Enter GUS.

GUS. Don't bother. It's only me.

He wears a white Palm Beach suit, hatless. HESTER *and* DAVID *stare at him in astonishment. She comes down the stairs. She is dressed in a robe, but has her best shoes on. Her hair is set.*

HESTER. Why, Gus! You look so handsome!

GUS. It is such a special day, I decided to make an impression on myself.

HESTER. No, you go perfectly with the room.

DAVID (*laughing with* GUS). Watch yourself or she'll hang you in a frame over the couch. (*He stamps at her to get her moving.*)

HESTER (*squealing, she runs to the stairs and up a few steps, and leans over the bannister*). Is your girl outside? Bring her in.

DAVID. Hey, that's right! Where's your girl?

GUS (*looking up*). Well, we both decided suddenly that until she can become as beautiful as Hester . . .

HESTER. Oh, you.

GUS (*opening his arms like a pleading lover*). Until she shows ability to make over a house like this was, and until etcetera and etcetera, she is not the girl for me, so I haven't seen her all week. Anyway, I have decided definitely I need only a red-headed girl.

HESTER (*to* GUS). Stand in the middle of the room when they come in. You make it look just like the picture in the Ladies Home Journal.

DAVID (*starting after her*). Get dressed, will ya? Dad'll cut my head off if we're not ready!

HESTER *laughs with delight and runs upstairs.*

GUS (*looking around*). It came out so nice. You know, this house shines in the sun a quarter of a mile away.

DAVID. Well, look at that sun! (*Goes right to windows.*) God must've pulled up the sun this morning, grabbed him by the back of the neck, and said – make it a baseball day.

GUS (*touching the wall*). Now it is truly a place to call home. Amazing.

DAVID (*laughs musingly, indicating the windows at the right*). You know, when I came down this morning that window caught my eye. I used to sneak under that window when we were kids and peek in here to watch Hester doing her homework. And then I used to sneak away. And now I can walk in and outa this house fifty times a day and sleep up in his room night after night! (*Looks through the window.*) Wherever he is I bet he still can't figure it out. Read the encyclopaedia if you like. I'll put on a tie. (*Goes to the landing.*)

GUS (*looking around*). Encyclopaedia, furniture, new plumbing. . . . When am I going to see a couple of brats around here!

DAVID (*stops at the landing*). What's the rush, you got some old suits you want ruined?

GUS. Me? I always pick up babies by the back of the neck, but . . . (*Idly.*) without children you wouldn't have to fix nothin' in here for twenty years. When nothing breaks it's boring. (*He sits, reaches over for an encyclopaedia volume.*)

DAVID (*glances above, comes away from stairs. Quietly*). I been wanting to ask you about that.

GUS. What?

DAVID (*hesitates. In good humour*). Did you ever hear of it happening when people didn't have kids because of the man?

GUS. Certainly, why not? Why don't you talk it over with her?

DAVID (*laughs self-consciously*). I can't seem to get around to it. I mean we somehow always took it for granted, kinda, that when the time was right a kid would just naturally come along.

GUS. You go to the doctor, then you'll know. . . . Or do you want to know?

DAVID. Sure I do, but I don't know it just doesn't seem *right*, especially when we've been all set financially for over two years now.

GUS. Right! What has this got to do with right or wrong? There is no justice in the world.

DAVID (*looks at him, then goes to the landing, stops*). I'll never believe that, Gus. If one way or another a man don't receive according to what he deserves inside . . . well, it's a madhouse.

HESTER (*from above*). There's a car stopping in front of the house! (*Coming down.*) Did you put your boots away?

DAVID (*slightly annoyed*). Yeh, I put 'em away! (*Goes across to the door.*)

HESTER (*hurrying downstairs*). You didn't! (*Hurrying across the room towards the boots.*) He'll have the place like a pigsty in a week!

DAVID *opens the door and looks out.*

GUS (*to* HESTER). Get used to it, the place will never be so neat once you have children around.

DAVID *turns to him, quickly, resentment in his face.*

HESTER (*stops moving. An eager glow lights up her expression. The boots are in her hand*). Don't you think it is a wonderful house for children?

DAVID. Hello! Hello, Mr Dibble! Didn't expect to see you around here today. Come in, come in.

Enter DAN DIBBLE *after wiping his feet carefully on the doormat.*

DIBBLE. Had to see J.B. on some business. Thought I'd stop in, say hello. Afternoon, Mrs Beeves.

HESTER. Hello, Mr Dibble. (*She picks up the boots and goes out.*)

DAVID. You know Gus Eberson. He's with me over at the shop.

DIBBLE. Sure, how are you, Gus? Say, you look more like a banker than a mechanic.

DAVID. Best mechanic there is.

DIBBLE. What I always say – never judge a man by his clothes. A man and his clothes are soon parted. (*They laugh.*) Say, J.B. was tellin' me you used to have a shop of your own here in town – over in Poplar Street was it . . . ?

DAVID. We amalgamated, Gus and I.

GUS. Actually, Mr Dibble, I ran out of money and customers after the first seven months. I am working now for Mr Beeves since over two years.

DIBBLE. Well, say, this is the first time I knew a hired man to insist he wasn't the boss's partner, and the boss to let on he was.

GUS (*chuckles*). Mr Beeves suffers sometimes from an over-developed sense of responsibility.

DIBBLE. That's why I spotted him as a natural mink man. Given it any more thought, David?

DAVID. A lot, Mr Dibble, a lot – but I'm afraid I haven't got an answer for you yet.

DIBBLE. Got time for a few facts today?

DAVID. Tell you the truth, we're expecting J.B. and Shory. Goin' up to Burley for the ball game. You heard about my brother, didn't you?

DIBBLE. J.B. said somethin' about him pitchin' against that coloured team. Say if he can knock them boys over he really belongs in the Big Leagues.

DAVID. I guess after today's game, Amos Beeves will be playin' for the Detroit Tigers.

DIBBLE. Well, say, they really took him, eh?

DAVID. Just about. A Tiger scout's goin' to be in the grandstand today.

DIBBLE. Well, say, it's about time.

DAVID. Yep, things even up, I guess in the long run. Why don't you drop around tonight. Havin' a big barbecue after the game.

Enter HESTER *from dining room.*

DIBBLE. Thanks, I'd like to but I got to get back and see my mink get fed on time and proper.

HESTER. David just never stops talkin' about mink. (*Sits.*) Have you still got that tiny one with the white spot on his head?

DAVID (*seeing* HESTER'*s interest, kindles a happy liveliness in him*). Oh, that one's probably been in and out of a dozen New York night clubs by this time. (*They laugh.*)

HESTER (*disturbed – to* DIBBLE). Oh, you didn't kill her?

DAVID (*to* GUS *and* HESTER). That's the way you get about mink, they're like people, little nervous people.

DIBBLE. I call them my little bankers myself. Pour a dollar's worth of feed down their gullets and they'll return you forty per cent; best little bankers in the world.

DAVID. Except when they fall, Mr Dibble, except when they fall.

DIBBLE. Mink never fall!

DAVID. Oh, now, Mr Dibble . . .

DIBBLE. They don't! It's their keepers fall down on them. When a feller goes broke tryin' to raise mink it's mainly because he's a careless man. From everything I've seen, David, you ain't that kind. You got a farm here clean as a hospital and mink needs a clean place. You're the first and only man I thought of when I decided to sell off some of my breeders when my doctor told me to ease up.

DAVID. I been askin' around lately, and everybody I talked to . . .

DIBBLE (*to* GUS *too*). I'm glad you made the inquiries. It shows you're a careful man. And now I'll tell you my answer. Easiest thing in the world is to kill a mink.

Mink'll die of a cold draught; they'll die of heart failure; indigestion can kill them, a cut lip, a bad tooth or sex trouble. And worse than that, the mink is a temperamental old woman. I wear an old brown canvas coat when I work around them. If I change that coat it might start them to eating their young. A big loud noise like thunder, or a heavy hailstorm comes and the mother's liable to pick up the litter, put 'em out in the open part of the cage, and then she'll go back into the nest box and close her eyes. As though they're out of danger if they're out of her sight. And when the storm's over you might have six or eight kits drowned to death out there. I've seen mink murder each other, I've seen them eat themselves to death and starve themselves to death, and I've seen them die of just plain worry. But! Not on my ranch! I'll show my records to anybody.

DAVID (*to* GUS). There's a business, boy!

GUS. A business! That's a slot machine. What do you need with mink?

DAVID. Oh, there's a kick in it, Gus. When you send a load of skins to New York you know you *did* something, you . . .

GUS. Why, you didn't do something? (*Indicates right.*) A great big shop you built up, a tractor station, how nice you made this farm . . . ?

DAVID (*not too intensely; he enjoys this talk*). Yeh, but is a thing really yours because your name is on it? Don't you have to feel you're smart enough, or strong enough, or something enough to have won it before it's really yours? You can't bluff a mink into staying alive. (*Turns to* DIBBLE.) I tell you, Mr Dibble . . .

DIBBLE. Take your time. Think about it . . .

DAVID. Let me call you. I'll let you know.

DIBBLE. Oh, I'll bide my time. Just remember, in New York they murder people for a mink coat. Women sell their jewels for mink, they sell their . . . them New York women'll sell damn near anything for mink!

They laugh, as horns of two cars sound urgently outside.

DAVID (*to* DIBBLE). This is my brother!

GUS (*as* DAVID *opens the door*). Look, like two peacocks!

HESTER (*at the door, over her shoulder ecstatically to* DIBBLE).
They've waited so long!

DAVID (*exuberantly, backing from the door*). Here he comes!
Christy Matthewson the Second!

Enter AMOS *and* PATTERSON *followed by* J.B..

HESTER (*grabbing* AMOS's *hand*). How's your arm, Ame!

AMOS (*winds up and pitches*). Wham! – He's out!

PAT (*throwing up his arms*). God bless this day! (*Suddenly.*)
I'm not waiting for anybody! (*Threatens to go out again.*)

J.B. (*to* HESTER). Shory's waiting in the car! Let's go!

HESTER. Bring him in. Let's have a drink!

Nobody hears her.

DAVID. What're you lookin' so sad about, Dad! (*Suddenly
hugs* PAT.)

HESTER. Get some whisky, Dave!

PAT (*indignantly – he has broken from* DAVE). You want to
suffocate in here? Open the windows in this house! (*He
rushes around throwing windows up.*)

DAVID (*laughing*). We're going in a minute! Where's the
telegram, Ame! (AMOS *opens his mouth but* PAT *cuts him
off.*)

PAT (*busy with the windows*). Let the day come in! What a
day! What a year! What a nation!

HESTER (*rushing after* PAT). Did you bring the telegram?
(*She corners him, laughing.*) Where's the telegram?

PAT. I don't need to bring it. I will never forget that telegram
so long as I live. (*Takes it out of his pocket.*) 'Western
Union. Class of Service. This is a full-rate Telegram or
Cablegram unless its deferred character is indicated by

a suitable symbol . . .'

HESTER. What're you reading that part for? (*Tries to grab it from him.*) What did the scout say!

PAT (*grabbing it back*). I'm reading it to you just the way I read it when I got it – from the very top, to the very bottom.

DAVID. Let him read it, Hess!

They go quiet.

PAT. I haven't felt this way since the last time I read the Bible. 'Patterson Beeves, 26 Murdock Street. Will be in Burley for the Black Giants game Sunday, July 16th. Looking forward to seeing Amos Beeves's performance. Best regards, Augie Belfast, Detroit Tigers. (*Looks around imperiously.*) Twenty-one years I have been waiting for this telegram. Training him down the cellar since he was old enough to walk. People laughed when Amos got bad marks in school. Forget the homework, I said. Keep your eye on the ball. Concentration, I said . . .

J.B. (*touched and fearing* PAT's *continuing indefinitely*). For God's sake, let's all have a drink!

DAVID. Comin' up! (*Goes out door.*)

HESTER (*pointing outside. To* J.B.). I'll bring Ellie in! Why don't you come to the game with us, Mr Dibble? (*She starts across to the door.*)

J.B. (*a little embarrassed, stops* HESTER). Better leave her, baby. You know how she is about alcohol. Let's not start anything.

GUS. Shory likes a drink. I'll bring him in. (*He goes out left.*)

PAT. Plenty of room in Dave's car, Mr Dibble. (*He studies* DIBBLE, *automatically massaging* AMOS's *arm.*)

J.B. (*holds his hand out to* HESTER). What do you think of this?

HESTER. A wedding ring! You giving Ellie a new ring?

J.B. (*warmly*). No, this is for me. Since we decided to adopt a baby I been feeling like we're newlyweds.

HESTER (*flings her arms around him*). You're such a silly man!

Enter SHORY, *pushed in by* GUS.

SHORY (*to* J.B.). Hey, Poppa, don't start nothin' you can't finish.

Enter DAVID *with drinks on a tray.*

HESTER (*three-quarters joking, but only that much. To* SHORY). And you've got a filthy mind.

SHORY. Madam, don't flatter me. (*To* DAVID, *who has been watching* HESTER *since* SHORY *came in.*) Hey, husband, where's that drink?

DAVID. Come on, everybody. Before we go! (*Gives out the drinks . . . Raises his glass.*) A toast! To everybody's luck – everybody's!

All raise their glasses.

GUS (*to* AMOS). And the next World's Series! (*Starts to drink.*)

DAVID. Wait! Make one big toast . . . to all our hearts' desires. For Amos! For Dad . . .

GUS. To David and Hester! To their prosperity, their shop, their tractor station, their farm . . .

DIBBLE (*suddenly struck with the idea*). And their mink!

HESTER (*quick complaint*). No . . .

DAVID (*he looks at* HESTER. *Her face softens toward him*). Not the mink now! From today on everything is coming true! To our children.

GUS. To their children.

J.B. Their children.

HESTER (*softly*). And in this year. Say that.

DAVID (*their eyes meet for an instant, and hold*). In this year . . . everything our hearts desire . . . *all of us*: in this year.

All drink.

PAT (*looks at watch*). Hey! We're late! We're getting drunk and the whole world is waiting for us out there! Come on!

They all rush out yelling and laughing as . . .

Curtain

Scene Two

Living Room. About seven o'clock that night.

The stage is empty. The gentle murmur and occasional laughter of the guests at the barbecue can be heard dimly. Presently, DAVID, followed by DAN DIBBLE come in through the front door. DAVID crosses to the desk and removes a large cheque book. He pauses over it, pen in hand.

DAVID. It's a fortune. I never wrote a cheque this big in my life.

DIBBLE. You never got so much for so little, David. You'll have prize stock, the finest breeding mink alive. The rest's up to you.

DAVID. Mr Dibble, I never thought I'd see my hand shaking.

The door at lower left opens and PAT appears. He closes the door gently behind him.

DAVID. Still asleep?

PAT. Shhh. I always make him take a long nap after a game.

DAVID. Aren't you going to eat anything?

PAT. I couldn't eat anything now. I'll eat after Belfast gets here. (*He sits on the couch.*) I was watchin' Amos just now asleep on the couch, and it suddenly struck me. Did you ever notice what a powerful face he has?

DAVID (*as he writes cheque*). He's great. After that game today there ain't a man in the world can doubt it. He's just great.

PAT. Didn't he look noble out there?

DAVID. Noble enough to vote for.

DAVID (*as he tears out cheque*). Here's your cheque, Mr Dibble. (DIBBLE *takes it.*)

DIBBLE. You'll never regret it, David.

DAVID. I hope not.

DIBBLE. Well, I'll be runnin' along now. You call me as soon as you get your cages ready and I'll bring 'em over. (DAVID *has walked him to the front door.*) Goodnight.

DAVID. G'night.

DIBBLE exits. DAVID *turns back into the room.*

PAT. You know why I'm extra glad? I think you were beginning to take it too hard, Dave. I was going to have a talk with you. Because I never had a doubt he'd scale the heights.

DAVID. I just didn't like the idea of me getting everything so steady, and him waiting around like . . . I mean you get to wondering if your own turn isn't coming.

PAT. Like what do you mean?

DAVID. A loss . . . a big unhappiness of some kind. But he's on his way now. I know it, Pop.

The door opens and J.B. *enters with a brand new valise. He is slightly drunk. In one hand he has a slip of paper.*

J.B. Surprise! (PAT *springs up with finger to his lips.*)

PAT. Shhh!

J.B. (*whispers*). Surprise! Wake him up. (*Pointing to valise.*) Surprise . . .

PAT. After a game he's got to sleep an hour or he's peevish. (*Pointing at watch.*) Wait a few minutes.

DAVID. Wait'll he sees the initials.

PAT (*violently*). Sssh! (*To* J.B. . . . *threatening.*) If he's peevish . . . !

The door opens and AMOS *stands in the doorway.*

J.B. Hey, Amos . . . (*Holding up valise.*) Surprise.

AMOS. Aw . . . ! (AMOS *takes the valise and fingers it happily.*)

J.B. It's a token of our affection from . . . just a minute now . . . (*Straightens the slip of paper.*) Hester, Shory, Gus, Dave, Ellie, and me, and Belle. (*Indicating upstage.*)

AMOS (*fondling the valise*). Gee, you should'na done it.

J.B. (*with growing flourish and sentiment*). No, you don't realize the travelling you'll do. (*Looks into the distance.*) Shibe Park, Commiskey Field, Sportsman's Park – Boston, Chicago, Cleveland, St Louis . . . And when you're packing up after a nice no-hitter, you'll give us a thought in the old home town. (*To clinch it, he taps a buckle.*) Solid brass.

AMOS (*feverish in glory, he gets up*). Give me that list. (*Takes it out of* J.B.'*s hand.*) When I get my first pay-cheque I'm gonna send you all a big present! Say . . . ! (*Starting to take* PAT'*s wrist to look at his watch.*) What time . . . ?

PAT (*holding onto his arm*). You heard what he said in the locker room. He's got to finish some long distance phoning, and then he'll be here. Come on. I'll rub you down.

HESTER *enters as they start for the stairs.*

HESTER. John, you better go outside. Ellie's going home.

J.B. (*frightened and hurt*). Why? (*To all.*) Am I so drunk?

DAVID. Hurry up, maybe you can catch her.

J.B. Come with me, Dave . . . tell her . . .

DAVID. Get washed, Ame . . . you want to look nice now. Be right back.

DAVID *and* J.B. *go out.*

HESTER (*looking at the door*). Why must he always do that?

(*To* PAT *who is rummaging in his old valise.*) I'll get you some towels. Come on up.

PAT. Oh, no, we carry our own. You never can tell about strange towels. (*He folds one over his arm.* AMOS *is looking out of the window.*)

HESTER (*ready to laugh*). Well, I wasn't going to give you a dirty towel, you stupid.

PAT. For twenty-one years I've kept him practically sterilized. I ain't layin' him low with an infection now. Come on, Amos, get washed.

AMOS *and* PAT *exit up the stairs as* J.B. *enters, followed by* DAVID. J.B. *is drunk, unsteady but not staggering. He barges in, comes directly to* HESTER *and takes her hand, speaks very close to her face, as though to discern her reactions better.*

J.B. Hester, you got to go home for me. (*He goes to window helplessly.*)

DAVID. Maybe she was only fooling, John . . .

J.B. No! But . . . (*To* HESTER.) Somebody's got to go home for me! (*And suddenly he bursts into uncontrolled sobbings.*)

HESTER. What in the world . . . !

DAVID (*angrily*). John! (*Shakes him, then seats him.*) John! Are you going to cut that out?

HESTER (*going to* J.B.). What happened? What did she say?

J.B. (*stops sobbing, sits swaying backwards, and forwards, very slightly in his chair*). All these years . . . we could've had children . . . all these weary, weary years.

HESTER. What are you talking about?

J.B. (*pointing waywardly towards the door to the outside*). Just told me . . . she made it up about the doctor . . . made it all up. We could've had two kids by now. (*Looks at* DAVID.) She wouldn't. She wouldn't. Because I drink, she says. A drunkard, she says! They'll wipe my name off my mail box like I never lived!

HESTER. Come upstairs and lie down. You make me so mad I could choke you! You could have everything in the world and you drink it away.

J.B. If I had a boy . . . I wouldn't have touched a drop.

HESTER. Oh, push! (*She tries to move him to the stairway.*)

J.B. I'm only a failure, Dave. The world is full of failures. All a man needs is one mistake and he's a failure.

DAVID *turns his head, a little annoyed.*

DAVID (*impatiently*). I know, John. (*Looks out window again.*)

J.B. You are the only man I ever knew who never makes a mistake. You understand me. Look at me! I am saying something.

DAVID (*now turns full to him*). What are you talking about?

J.B. I'm not as drunk as I look, David! You're a good man, yes. You know how to do. But you've had a phenomenal lot of luck in your life, Dave. Never play luck too hard. It's like a season, and seasons pass away.

HESTER. Come up or you'll pass away.

Enter PAT *downstairs with watch in hand.*

PAT. My watch says eight-thirty, where is he? He told you no later than eight o'clock, didn't he?

DAVID. Which means he's half an hour late. That's what it means, doesn't it?

PAT. I don't know what to tell Amos. I made him take another shower.

DAVID (*with growing fear*). He pitched the greatest game of his life today, what more does he need to be told? That man'll be here.

PAT. Maybe he was kidding us. He looked like he might be that type.

DAVID. Are you going to stop that?

PAT. . . . And Amos did look a little nervous in the eighth inning with those two men on base.

DAVID. But they didn't score! Now will you just stop.

PAT, *hurt, looks at him, then goes to the stairs.*

Dad, what you want me to do; I can't grow him in my back yard, can I?

SHORY *enters pushed by* GUS. *At the stairs,* PAT *turns, starts to speak, then goes up and out.*

SHORY (*as the door shuts*). I'm getting my aches and pains. I came in to say goodnight . . . Party's breakin' up anyway out there.

DAVID. No, wait a little. I don't want everybody pulling out. (*He goes to window as . . .*)

SHORY. The man told you seven-thirty, what're you making believe he said eight? You told me as he said seven-thirty, didn't you?

DAVID (*his fury is at the scout. He keeps searching out of the window*). He could've got a flat maybe.

SHORY. It don't take an hour to change a flat, Dave.

DAVID (*tensely. He turns*). Don't go away. Please.

Enter HESTER.

(*To* HESTER.) The folks are starting to go. (*Moving her back to the door.*) I want a party here when the scout leaves. Keep them here.

HESTER. It's not the world coming to an end. I don't want you acting this way. It's no fault of yours what happens to him. (*She grasps him.*) Why do you act this way? Davey . . .

DAVID. I don't get it, I swear to God I don't get it. (*Strides to the window. He seems about to burst from the room.*)

SHORY. Get what?

DAVID. Everything is so hard for him. (*Turns to them suddenly, unable to down his anxiety.*) I want to ask you something. All of you, and you too, Hess. You know what I can do and what I can't do, you . . . you know me. Everything I touch, why is it? It turns gold. Everything.

HESTER. What's come over you? Why . . .?

DAVID (*with extreme urgency*). It bothers me, it . . . (*To all.*) What is it about me? I never . . . I never lose. Since we were kids I expected Amos to rise and shine. He's the one, he knows something, he knows one thing perfect. Why? Is it all luck? Is that what it is?

GUS. Nonsense. You're a good man, David.

DAVID. Aren't you good?

GUS. Yes, but I . . .

DAVID. Then why did your shop fail? Why are you working for me now? (*He moves as one in the throes of release.*)

GUS. They remember the war here, Dave, they don't like to buy from a foreigner.

DAVID. No, that's crazy.

GUS. Also, I had a second-rate location.

DAVID. Gus, it was better than mine. Every car coming into town had to pass your place. And they came to me. Why is that?

GUS. You know an engine, Dave, you . . .

DAVID. Including Marmons? (*To all.*) I got fourteen thousand dollars in the bank and as much again standing on the ground. Amos? Never had a nickel. Not a bloody nickel. Why?

A slight pause.

HESTER (*goes to him. Smiles to make him smile but he does not*). Why does it bother you? It's good to be lucky. Isn't it?

DAVID (*looks at her a moment*). Isn't it better to feel that what you have came to you because of something special you can do? Something, something . . . inside you? Don't you have to know what that thing is?

HESTER. Don't you know?

DAVID. . . . I don't, I don't know.

SHORY. And you'll never know . . .

DAVID. Damn it all, if everything drops on you like fruit from a tree, for no reason, why can't it break away for no reason? Everything you have . . . suddenly.

HESTER (*takes* DAVID's *arm*). Come, say goodbye to the folks.

DAVID. No . . . they're not going home till the scout comes! Now go out . . .

HESTER (*shakes his arm*). It's his hard luck, not yours!

DAVID. It is mine! A man has a right to get what he deserves. He does, damn it! (*He goes to the window, breaking from her.*)

HESTER (*angrily*). You talk like you'd stole something from him. You never got anything you didn't deserve. You . . .

DAVID (*at the end of his patience, he turns on her*). Am I that good and he that bad? I can't believe it. There's something wrong, there's something wrong! (*Suddenly.*) I'm going to Burley. (*To* HESTER, *hurriedly.*) Where's the keys to the car . . . ?

HESTER. You don't even know where to find the man . . .

DAVID. I'll find him, where are the keys?

HESTER (*she grabs him*). Davey, stop it . . .

DAVID. I'm going, I'll drag him here . . . !

HESTER (*fright*). Davey . . . !

He strides towards the door. SHORY *grabs his arm and holds it fast.*

SHORY. Stop it!

DAVID. Let go of me!

SHORY (*he will not let go*). Listen to me, you damn fool! There's nothing you can do, you understand?

DAVID. Let go of my arm . . .

SHORY (*forces him down into a chair*). David, I'm going to tell you something . . . I never told you before. But you need to know this now. Amos deserves better than this, but I deserved better than this too. (*Pats his thighs.*) When I went to France there was no broken bones in my imagination. I left this town with a beautiful moustache and full head of hair. Women travelled half the state to climb into my bed. Even over there, under shot and shell, as they say, there was a special star over my head. I was the guy nothin' was ever going to hit . . . And nothin' ever did, David. (*He releases* DAVID's *arm. Now* DAVID *does not move away.*) Right through the war without a scratch. Surprised? I walked into Paris combing my hair. The women were smiling at me from both sides of the street, and I walked up the stairs with the whistles blowing out the Armistice. I remember how she took off my shoes and put them under the bed. The next thing I knew the house was laying on my chest and they were digging me out.

DAVID, *all, stare at him.*

HESTER. Everybody said it was a battle, I thought . . .

SHORY (*to her*). No, no battle at all. (*To* DAVID.) In battle – there's almost a reason for it, a man almost 'deserves' it that way. I just happened to pick out the one woman in Paris who lived in a house where the janitor was out getting drunk on the Armistice. He forgot to put water in the furnace boiler. (*Smiles.*) The walls blew out. (*Points upstage with his thumb over his shoulder.*) Amos's walls happened to blow out. And you happen to be a lucky boy, brother David. A jellyfish can't swim no matter how he tries; it's the tide that pushes him every time. So just keep feeding, and enjoy the water till you're thrown up on the beach to dry.

Pause.

HESTER (*goes to him*). Come, Dave, the folks are waiting to say goodbye.

DAVID *is forced to turn quickly towards the window. It is an indecisive turn of the head, a questioning turn and she follows as he strides to the window and looks out towards upstage direction . . .*

DAVID. Wait! (*Starting for the window.*) A car? (*Turns quickly to them all.*) It didn't go past. It stopped. (*He starts quickly for the door, across the stage, right.* PAT *rushes down the stairs.*)

PAT. He's here! He came! Get out, everybody! (*To all.*) All the way from Burley in a taxicab! Dave, you stay. I want your advice when he starts talkin' contract! (PAT *rushes out.*)

DAVID (*as they all keep exclaiming*). Out, out, all of you! (*As they start for door,* DAVID *musses* SHORY). Where's your jellyfish now, brother!

SHORY (*at door with the others*). His luck is with him, sister, that's all, his luck!

DAVID. Luck, heh? (*Smiling, he bends over* SHORY, *pointing left toward his big desk and speaking privately . . .*) Some day remind me to open the middle drawer of that desk. I'll show you a fistful of phone bills for calls to Detroit.

GUS (*joyously*). Dave. You called them!

DAVID. Sure, I called them. That man is here because I brought him here! (*To* SHORY.) Where's the jellyfish could've done that! (*Triumphantly, to all.*) Don't anybody go. We're going to raise the roof tonight!

They have all gone out now, on his last lines. Only HESTER *remains in the doorway.*

DAVID *looks at her a moment, and with a laugh embraces her quickly.*

I'll tell you everything he says.

HESTER. Be like this all the time, Davey. (*She turns toward the hallway into which this door leads.*) Tell me every word, now. (*She goes.*)

DAVID *quickly brushes his hair back, looking rapidly about the room and to himself . . .*

DAVID. Now it's wonderful: This is how it ought to be!

Enter AMOS – *comes downstairs.*

AMOS (*hushed, with his hands clasped as though in prayer*). God, it's happening just like it ought've. 'Cause I'm good. I betcha I'm probably great! (*He says this, facing the door, glancing at* DAVID.)

Enter AUGIE BELFAST *and* PAT. AUGIE *is a big Irishman dressed nattily.*

PAT (*as they enter*). . . . . couldn't stop him from setting up a party. (*Sees* DAVE.) Oh, here he is.

AUGIE (*to* AMOS *and* DAVID.). Sit down, sit down. Don't stand on ceremony with me. I'm Augie Belfast . . .

AMOS *sits on the bed.* DAVID *in a chair. As* PAT . . .

PAT. Let me have your coat?

AUGIE (*lays down his hat*). It don't bother me. I live in it. Thanks just the same. (*Taking out chewing gum.*) Gum?

DAVID. No thanks, we've been eating all day . . . mean

AUGIE (*unfolding a slice as* PAT *sits. He moves about constantly; he already has a wad of gum in his cheek*). Loosen up, don't stand in awe of me. (*To* DAVID *and* AMOS.) I was just telling your father . . . I got tied up in Burley on some long-distance calls. I'm very sorry to be so late. (*He is anxious to be pardoned.*)

DAVID. Oh, that's all right. We know how busy you fellas are.

AUGIE. Thanks. I knew how you must've been feeling. (*He paces a little, chewing, looking at the floor.*) Amos? (*He says nothing for a long moment. Stops walking, looks down, slowly unfolds another slice of gum.*)

AMOS (*whisper*). Ya?

AUGIE. Amos, how long you been pitchin'?

AMOS. Well, about . . . (*Turns to* PAT.)

PAT. Steadily since he's been nine years old.

AUGIE (*nods. Pause*). I guess you know he's a damn fine

pitcher.

PAT (*comfortably*). We like to think so around here.

AUGIE. Yeh, he's steady, he's good. Got a nice long arm, no nerves in that arm. He's all right. He feels the plate. (*All the time thinking of something else, pacing.*)

PAT. Well, you see, I've had him practicing down the cellar against a target. Dug the cellar out deeper so he could have room after he grew so tall.

AUGIE. Yeh, I know. Man sitting next to me this afternoon was telling me. Look, Mr Beeves . . . (*He straddles a chair, folds his arms on its back, facing them.*) I want you to have confidence in what I say. I'm Augie Belfast, if you know anything about Augie Belfast you know he don't bull. There's enough heartbreak in this business without bull-throwers causin' any more. *In toto*, I don't string an athlete along. Pitchin' a baseball to me is like playin' the piano well, or writin' beautiful literature, so try to feel I'm giving you the last word because I am. (PAT *nods a little, hardly breathing.*) I have watched many thousands of boys, Mr Beeves. I been whackin' the bushes for material for a long time. You done a fine job on Amos. He's got a fine, fast ball, he's got a curve that breaks off sharp, he's got his control down to a pinpoint. He's almost original sometimes. When it comes to throwin' a ball, he's all there. Now. (*Slight pause.*) When I saw him two years ago, I said . . .

DAVID (*electrically*). You were *here* before?

AUGIE. Oh yeh, I meant to tell you. I came to see him last year, too . . .

PAT. Why didn't you let me know?

AUGIE. Because there was one thing I couldn't understand, Mr Beeves. I understand it today, but I couldn't then. When the bases are clear, Mr Beeves, and there's nobody on, your boy is terrific . . . Now wait a minute, let me say rather that he's good, very good . . . I don't want to say an untruth, your boy is good when nobody's on. But as soon as a man gets on base and starts rubbin' his spikes in the dirt and makin' noise behind your boy's back, something happens to him. I seen it once, I seen it twice, I seen it every time the bases get loaded. And once the crowd starts howlin', your boy, Mr Beeves, is floatin' somewhere out in paradise.

PAT. But he pitched a shut-out.

AUGIE. Only because them Black Giants like to swing bats. If they'd waited him out in the eighth inning they could've walked in half a dozen runs. Your boy was out of control. (*Dead silence.*) I couldn't understand it. I absolutely couldn't get the angle on it. Here's a boy with a terrific . . . Well, let's not say terrific, let's say a damn good long arm. But not an ounce of base-brains. There is something in him that prevents him from playin' the bases . . .

PAT. I know, I've been drilling him the last three years.

AUGIE. I know, but in three years there's been no improvement. In fact, this year he's worse in that respect than last year. Why? Today I found the answer.

PAT (*softly*). You did?

AUGIE. The guy sitting next to me mentions about him pitchin' down the cellar since he was nine years old. That was it! Follow me now. In the cellar there is no crowd. In the cellar he knows exactly what's behind his back. In the cellar, *in toto*, your boy is home. He's only got to concentrate on that target, his mind is trained to take in that one object, just the target. But once he gets out on a wide ball field, and a crowd is yelling in his ears, and there's two or three men on bases jumpin' back and forth behind him his mind has got to do a lot of things at once, he's in a strange place, he gets panicky, he gets paralyzed, he gets mad at the base runners and he's through! From that minute he can't pitch worth a nickel bag of cold peanuts!

He gets up, pulls down his vest. DAVID *and* PATTERSON *sit dumbly,* AMOS *staring at nothing.*

I got to make a train, Mr Beeves.

PAT (*slowly rises. As though in a dream*). I didn't want to waste the winters, that's why I trained him down the cellar.

AUGIE (*thoughtfully*). Yeh, that's just where you made your mistake, Mr Beeves.

DAVID (*rises*). But . . . that was his plan. He didn't want to waste the winters. Down the cellar . . . it seemed like such a good idea!

AUGIE. But it was a mistake.

DAVID. But he's been doing it twelve years! A man can't be multiplying the same mistake for twelve years, can he?

AUGIE. I guess he can, son. It was a very big mistake.

Pause.

PAT. Well . . . you can't take that out of him? Your coaches and . . . everything?

AUGIE. There's no coach in the world can take out a boy's brain and set it back twelve years. Your boy is crippled up here. (*Taps his temple.*) I'm convinced.

DAVID. But if you coached him right, if you drilled him day after day . . .

AUGIE. It would take a long, long time, and I personally don't believe he'll ever get rid of it.

PAT. You can't . . . you can't try him, eh?

AUGIE. I know how you feel, Mr Beeves, but I am one man who will not take a boy out of his life when I know in my heart we're going to throw him away like a wet rag.

DAVID (*for a long time he stands staring*). He has no life.

AUGIE (*bends closer to hear*). Eh?

DAVID. He doesn't know how to do anything else.

AUGIE (*nods with sympathy*). That was another mistake. (*He starts to turn away to go.*)

PAT (*as though to call him back somehow*). I believed if he concentrated . . . concentration . . . you see I myself always jumped from one thing to another and never got anywhere, and I thought . . .

AUGIE. Yeh . . . when it works concentration is a very sound principle. (*Takes a breath.*) Well, lots of luck.

Still unable to believe, PAT *can't speak.*

'Bye, Amos.

AMOS *nods slightly, numbly staring. At the door, to* DAVE.

'Bye. (*He starts to open the door.*)

DAVID. Look . . . (*He hurries to him. He looks in his eyes, his hand raised as though to grab the man and hold him here.*)

AUGIE. Yeh?

DAVID *starts to speak, then looks at* AMOS *who is still staring at nothing.* DAVID *turns back to* AUGIE

DAVID. . . You'll see him in the Leagues.

AUGIE. I hope so. I just don't . . .

DAVID (*trying to restrain his fury*). No, you'll see him. You're not the only team, you know. You'll see him in the Leagues.

AUGIE (*grasps* DAVID'*s arm*). . . . . Take it easy, boy. (*To the others.*) I hope you'll pardon me for being late.

DAVID (*quietly, like an echo, his voice cracking*). You'll see him.

AUGIE *nods. Glances at* PAT *and* AMOS, *opens the door and goes.* PAT *and* DAVID *stand looking at the door.* PAT *turns now, walks slowly to* AMOS *who is sitting. As* PAT *nears him he stands slowly, his fists clenched at his sides.*

PAT (*softly, really questioning*). He can be wrong too, can't he? (AMOS *is silent, his face filling with hate.*) Can't he be wrong? (*No reply.*) He can, can't he?

AMOS (*a whip-like shout*). No, he can't be!

PAT. But everybody makes mistakes . . .

AMOS (*with a cry he grabs* PAT *by the collar and shakes him violently back and forth*). Mistakes! Mistakes! You and your goddam mistakes!

DAVID (*leaps to them, trying to break his grip*). Let him go! Amos, let him go!

AMOS (*amid his own, and* PAT'*s weeping. To* PAT). You liar! I'll kill you, you little liar, *you liar!*

With a new burst of violence he starts forcing PAT *backward and down to the floor.* GUS *comes in as* DAVID *locks an arm around* AMOS'*s neck and jerks him from* PAT *who falls to the floor.*

Leave me alone! Leave me alone!

With a great thrust DAVID *throws* AMOS *to the couch and stands over him, fists raised.* HESTER *unnoticed enters and stands watching the scene.*

DAVID. Stay there! Don't get up! You'll fight me, Amos!

PAT (*scurrying to his feet, and taking* DAVID *away from the couch*). Don't, don't fight! (*He turns quickly, pleadingly to* AMOS, *who is beginning to sob on the couch.*) Amos, boy, boy . . . (AMOS *lies across the couch and sobs violently.* PAT *leans over and pats his head.*) Boy, boy . . .

AMOS *swings his arm out blindly and hits* PAT *across the chest.* DAVID *starts toward them but* PAT *remains over him, patting his back.*

Come on, boy, please, boy, stop now, stop, Amos! look, Ame, look, I'll get Cleveland down here, I'll go myself, I'll bring a man. Ame, listen, I did what I could, a man makes mistakes, he can't figure on everything . . . (*He begins shaking* AMOS *who continues sobbing.*) Ame, stop it! (*He stands and begins shouting over* AMOS'*s sobbing.*) I admit it, I admit it, Ame, I lie, I talk too much, I'm a fool, I admit it, but look how you pitch, give me credit for that, give me credit for something! (*Rushes at* AMOS *and turns him over.*) Stop that crying! God Almighty, what do you want me to do! I'm a fool, what can I do!

DAVID (*wrenches* PAT *away from the couch. Stands over* AMOS). Listen, you! (*Leans over and pulls* AMOS *by the collar to a sitting position.* AMOS *sits limply, sobbing.*) He made a mistake. That's over with. You're going to drill on base play. You got a whole life. One mistake can't ruin a life. He'll go to Cleveland. I'll send him to New York . . .

HESTER *enters quietly.*

The man can be wrong. Look at me! The man can be wrong, you understand!

AMOS *shakes his head.*

AMOS. He's right.

DAVID *releases him and stands looking down at him.* AMOS *gets up slowly, goes to a chair and sits.*

He's right. I always knew I couldn't play the bases. Everything the man said was right. I'm dumb, that's why. I can't figure nothin'. (*Looks up at* PAT.) There wasn't no time, he said, no time for nothin' but throwin' that ball. Let 'em laugh, he said, you don't need to know how to figure. He knew it all. He knows everything! Well, this is one time I know something. I ain't gonna touch a baseball again as long as I live!

PAT (*frantically*). Amos, you don't know what you're saying . . . !

AMOS. I couldn't ever stand out on a diamond again! I can't do it! I know! I can't! (*Slight pause.*) I ain't goin' to let you kid me any more. I'm through. (*He rises.* PAT *sobs into his hands.*)

DAVID (AMOS *keeps shaking his head in denial of everything*). What do you mean, through? Amos, you can't lay down.

Listen to me. Stop shaking your head – who gets what he wants in this world!!

AMOS (*suddenly*). You. Only you.

DAVID. Me! Don't believe it, Amos. (*Grabs him.*) Don't believe that any more!

AMOS. Everything you ever wanted . . . in your whole life, every . . . !

DAVID. Including my children, Ame? (*Silence.*) Where are my children!

HESTER. Dave . . .

DAVID (*to* HESTER). I want to tell him! (*To* AMOS.) What good is everything when nothing is good without children? Do you know the laughing stock it makes of everything you do in the world? You'll never meet a man who doesn't carry one curse . . . at least one. Shory, J.B., Pop, you, and me too. Me as much as anybody!

HESTER. Don't, Davey . . .

DAVID (*with a dreadful triumph*). No, Hess, I'm not afraid of it any more. I want it out. I was always afraid I was something special in the world. But not after this. (*To* AMOS.) *Nobody* escapes, Ame! But I don't lay down, I don't die because I'll have no kids. A man is born with one curse at least to be cracked over his head. I see it now, and you got to see it. Don't envy me, Ame . . . we're the same now. The world is made that way, as if a law was written in the sky somewhere – nobody escapes! (*Takes* AMOS's *hand.*)

HESTER (*almost weeping she cannot restrain*). Why do you talk that way?

DAVID. Hess, the truth . . .

HESTER. It's not the truth! . . . You have no curse! None at all!

DAVID (*struck*). What . . .?

HESTER. I wanted to wait till the scout signed him up. And then . . . when the house was full of noise and cheering, I'd stand with you on the stairs high over them all, and tell them you were going to have a child. (*With anger and disappointment and grief.*) Oh Davey, I saw you so proud . . . !

DAVID (*twisted and wracked, he bursts out*). Oh, Hess, I am, I am.

HESTER. No, you don't want it. I don't know what's happened to you, you don't want it now!

DAVID (*with a chill of horror freezing him*). Don't say that! Hester, you mustn't . . . (DAVID *tries to draw her to him.*)

HESTER (*holding him away*). You've got to want it, Davey. You've just got to want it!

She bursts into tears and rushes out. He starts after her, calling her name . . . when he finds himself facing AMOS.

AMOS. Nobody escapes . . . (DAVID *stops, turns to* AMOS.) . . . except you. (*He walks to the door, past* DAVID *and goes out.*)

Curtain.

ACT THREE

Scene One

Living room. Night in the following February.

J.B. is asleep on the couch. SHORY *and* GUS *are silently playing cards and smoking at a table near the fireplace. Snow can be seen on the window muntins. Several coats on the rack. Presently . . .*

GUS. There's no brainwork in this game. Let me teach you claviash.

SHORY. I can win all the money I need in rummy and pinochle. Play.

GUS. You have no intellectual curiosity.

SHORY. No, but you can slip me a quarter. (*Showing his hand.*) Rummy.

Enter BELLE *from the stairs.*

GUS (*to* BELLE). Everything all right?

BELLE (*half turns to him, holding blanket forth*). She keeps sweating up all the blankets. That poor girl.

GUS. The doctor says anything?

BELLE. Yes . . . (*Thinks.*) . . . he said, go down and get a dry blanket.

GUS. I mean, about when it will be coming along?

BELLE. Oh, you can't tell about a baby. That's one thing about them, they come most any time. Sometimes when you don't expect it, and sometimes when you do expect it. (*She goes up to door and turns again.*) Why don't Davey buy a baby carriage?

GUS. Didn't he? I suppose he will.

BELLE. But how can you have a baby without a baby

carriage?

SHORY. You better blow your nose.

BELLE. I haven't time! (*She blows her nose and goes out, up left.*)

SHORY. A quarter says it's a boy. (*Tosses a quarter on the table.*)

GUS. It's a bet. You know, statistics show more girls is born than boys. You should've asked me for odds.

SHORY. Dave Beeves doesn't need statistics, he wants a boy. Matter of fact, let's raise it – a dollar to your half that he's got a boy tonight.

GUS. Statistically I would take the bet, but financially I stand pat.

Enter DAVID *from left door to outside. He is dressed for winter. It is immediately evident that a deep enthusiasm, a ruddy satisfaction is upon him. He wears a strong smile. He stamps his feet a little as he removes his gloves, and then his short coat, muffler, hat, leaving a sweater on. As he closes the door.*

DAVID. How'm I doing upstairs?

GUS. So far she only sweats.

DAVID. Sweating! Is that normal?

GUS. Listen she ain't up there eating ice cream.

DAVID (*goes to the fireplace, rubs his hands before it. Of* J.B. *as though amused*). The least little thing happens and he stays home from work. He's been here all day.

GUS. Certain men like to make holidays. A new kid to him is always a holiday.

DAVID (*he looks around*). What a fuss.

GUS. You're very calm. Surprising to me. Don't you feel nervous?

SHORY (*to* GUS). You seen too many movies. What's the use of him pacing up and down?

DAVID (*with an edge of guilt*). I got the best doctor; everything she needs. I figure, whatever's going to happen'll happen. After all, I can't . . .

Breaks off. In a moment BELLE *enters from the left door, carrying a different blanket. She goes toward the stair landing.* DAVID *finally speaks, unable to restrain it.*

Belle . . . (*She stops. He goes to her, restraining anxiety.*) Would you ask the Doctor . . . if he thinks it's going to be very hard for her, heh?

BELLE. He told me to shut up.

DAVID. Then ask J.B.'s wife.

BELLE. She told me to shut up too. But I'll ask her.

BELLE *goes up the stairs.* DAVID *watches her ascend a moment.*

DAVID (*looking upstairs*). That girl is going to live like a queen after this. (*Turns to them, banging his fist in his palm.*) Going to make a lot of money this year.

SHORY. Never predict nothin' but the weather, half an hour ahead.

DAVID. Not this time. I just finished mating my mink, and I think every one of them took.

GUS. All finished? That's fine.

A knock is heard on the door. DAVID *goes to it, opens it.* PAT *enters. He is dressed in a pea jacket, a stocking wool hat on his head. He carries a duffle bag on his shoulder.*

DAVID. Oh, hello, Dad.

PAT. The baby come yet?

DAVID. Not yet.

PAT. My train doesn't leave for a couple of hours. I thought I'd wait over here.

DAVID. Here, give me that. (*He takes the duffle bag from* PAT, *puts it out of the way.*)

SHORY. So you're really going, Pat?

PAT. I got my old job back – ship's cook. I figure with a little studying, maybe in a year or so, I'll have my Third license. So . . .

DAVID. It's so foolish your leaving, Dad. Can't I change your mind?

PAT. It's better this way, David. Maybe if I'm not around Amos'll take hold of himself.

There is a knock on the door.

DAVID. That's probably Amos now.

He goes to the door, opens it. AMOS *enters. He is smoking a cigarette.*

Hello, Ame. All locked up? Come in.

AMOS. I got my motor running. Hello, Gus, Shory. (*He ignores* PAT. *There is a pause.*)

GUS. Working hard?

AMOS (*a tired, embittered chuckle*). Yeh, pretty tough; pumpin' gas, ringin' the cash register . . . (*Giving* DAVID *a small envelope and a key.*) There's twenty-six bucks in there. I got the tally slip in with it.

DAVID (*as though anxious for his participation; strained*). Twenty-six! We did all right today.

AMOS. Always do, don't ya? 'Night. (*Starts to go.*)

DAVID. Listen, Ame. (AMOS *turns.*) The mink'll be bearing in about a month. I was thinking you might like to take a shot at working with me, here . . . it's a great exercise . . . Spring is coming, you know. You want to be in condition . . .

AMOS. For what?

DAVID. Well . . . maybe play some ball this summer.

AMOS (*glances at* PAT). Who said I'm playing ball?

DAVID (*as carelessly as possible*). What are you going to do with yourself?

AMOS. Pump your gas . . . Bring you the money every night. Wait for something good to happen. (*A bitter little laugh.*) I mean the day they announced they're building the new main highway right past your gas station I knew *something* good had to happen to me. (*Laughing.*) I mean it just *had* to, Dave! (*Now with real feeling.*) Baby hasn't come yet? (DAVID *shakes his head, disturbed by his brother's bitterness.*) Overdue, ain't she? (*Takes a drag on his cigarette.*)

DAVID. A little.

AMOS. Well, if it's a boy . . . (*Glancing at* PAT *and defiantly blowing out smoke.*) Don't have him pitchin' down the cellar.

With a wink at DAVID, *he goes out. After a moment* DAVID *goes to* PAT.

DAVID. Why must you go, Dad? Work with me here, I've plenty for everybody, I don't need it all.

PAT. Inhaling cigarettes in those glorious lungs. I couldn't bear to watch him destroying my work that way.

SHORY (*at the fireplace*). Come on, Pat, pinochle.

DAVID (*beckoning* GUS *over to the right*). Hey, Gus, I want to talk to you.

PAT (*going to* SHORY. *Without the old conviction*). Fireplace heat is ruination to the arteries.

PAT *takes* GUS's *place,* GUS *coming to the right.*

SHORY (*mixing the deck*). So you'll drop dead warm. Sit down. (*He deals.*)

DAVID *and* GUS *are at right.* J.B. *continues sleeping. The card game begins.*

DAVID. I want you to do something for me, Gus. In a little more than thirty days I'll have four or five mink for every bitch in those cages. Four to one.

GUS. Well, don't count the chickens . . .

DAVID. No, about this I'm sure. I want to mortgage the shop. Before you answer . . . I'm not being an Indian giver. I signed sixty percent of the shop over to you because you're worth it – I didn't want what don't belong to me and I still don't. I just want you to sign so I can borrow some money on the shop. I need about twenty-five hundred dollars.

GUS. I can ask why?

DAVID. Sure. I want to buy some more breeders.

GUS. Oh. Well, why not use the money you have?

DAVID. Frankly, Gus . . . (*Laughs confidently.*) . . . I don't have any other money.

GUS. Ah, go on now, don't start kidding me . . .

DAVID. No, it's the truth. I've damn near as many mink out there as Dan Dibble. That costs big money. What do you say?

PAT *and* SHORY *look up now and listen while playing their hands.*

GUS (*thinks a moment*). Why do you pick on the shop to mortgage? You could get twenty-five hundred on the gas station, or the quarry, or the farm . . . (*Slight pause.*)

DAVID. I did. I've got everything mortgaged. Everything but the shop.

GUS (*shocked*). Dave I can't believe this!

DAVID (*indicates out of the right window*). Well, look at them out there. I've got a *ranch*. You didn't think I had enough cash to buy that many, did you?

GUS (*gets up trying to shake off his alarm*). But, Dave, this is mink. Who knows what can happen to them? I don't understand how you can take everything you own and sink it in . . .

DAVID. Four for one, Gus. If prices stay up I can make sixty thousand dollars this year.

GUS. But how can you be sure; you can't . . .

DAVID. I'm sure.

GUS. But how can you be . . . ?

DAVID (*more nervously now, wanting to end this tack*). I'm sure. Isn't it possible? To be sure?

GUS. Yes, but why? (*Pause.*) Why are you sure?

J.B. (*suddenly erupting on the couch*). Good Good and . . . ! (*He sits up rubbing himself.*) What happened to those radiators you were going to put into this house? (*He gets up, goes to the fire, frozen.*) You could hang meat in this room.

DAVID (*to* J.B.). You're always hanging meat.

GUS. I don't know how to answer you. I have worked very hard in the shop . . . I . . . (*His reasonableness breaks.*) You stand there and don't seem to realize you'll be wiped out if those mink go, and now you want more yet!

DAVID. *I said they're not going to die!*

J.B. (*to* PAT *and* SHORY). Who's going to die? What're they talking about?

DAVID. Nothin'. (*He looks out of the window.* J.B. *watches him, mystified.*)

PAT. I think Amos would smoke a pipe instead of those cigarettes, if you told him, Shory.

J.B. Dave, you want a baby carriage y'know.

DAVID (*half turns*). Heh? . . . Yey, sure.

J.B. I figured you forgot to ask me so I ordered a baby carriage for you.

DAVID *turns back to the window as* . . .

Matter of fact, it's in the store. (*With great enthusiasm.*) Pearl grey! Nice soft rubber tyres too . . . boy, one thing I love to see . . .

DAVID (*turns to him, restraining*). All right, will you stop talking?

J.B. *is shocked. In a moment he turns and goes to the rack, starts getting into his coat.* DAVID *crosses quickly to him.*

Oh, John, what the hell! (*He takes* J.B.*'s arm.*)

J.B. You unnerve me, Dave! You unnerve me! A man acts a certain way when he's going to be a father, and by Jesus I want him to act that way.

SHORY. Another movie-goer! Why should he worry about something he can't change?

DAVID. I've got a million things to think of, John. I want to ask you.

J.B. What?

DAVID (*hangs* J.B.'s *coat up*). I want to get a buy on a new Buick; maybe you can help me swindle that dealer you know in Burley. I'm taking Hester to California in about a month. Sit down.

J.B. (*suddenly pointing at him*). That's what unnerves me! You don't seem to realize what's happening. You can't take a month old baby in a car to California.

DAVID (*a blank, shocked look*). Well, I meant . . .

J.B. (*laughs, slaps his back relieved at this obvious truth*). The trouble with you is, you don't realize that she didn't swell up because she swallowed an olive! (GUS *and he laugh;* DAVID *tries to.*) You're a poppa, boy! You're the guy he's going to call Pop!

There is a commotion of footsteps upstairs. DAVID *goes quickly to the landing.* BELLE *hurries down. She is sniffling, sobbing.*

DAVID. What happened?

BELLE *touches his shoulder kindly but brushes right past him to the fireplace where she picks up a wood basket.*

(DAVID *continues going to her.*) What happened, Belle!

BELLE (*standing with the wood*). She's having it, she's having it. (*She hurries to the landing,* DAVID *behind her.*)

DAVID. What does the doctor say? Belle! How is she? (*He catches her arm.*)

BELLE. I don't know. She shouldn't have fallen that time. She shouldn't have fallen, Davey. Oh dear . . .

She bursts into a sob and rushes upstairs. DAVID *stands gaping upwards. But* GUS *is staring at* DAVID. *After a long moment . . .*

GUS (*quietly*). Hester fell down?

DAVID (*turns slowly to him after an instant of his own*). What?

GUS. Hester had a fall?

DAVID. Yeh, some time ago.

GUS. You had her to the doctor?

DAVID. Yeh.

GUS. He told you the baby would be possibly dead? (*Pause.*)

DAVID. What're you talking about?

GUS (*quavering*). I think you know what I'm talking about.

DAVID *is speechless. Walks to a chair and sits on the arm as though, at the price of terrible awkwardness, to simulate ease. Always glancing at* GUS, *he gets up unaccountably, and in a broken, uncontrolled voice . . .*

DAVID. What are you talking about?

GUS. I understand why you were so sure about the mink. But I sign no mortgage on the shop. I do not bet on dead children.

DAVID *is horrified at the revelation. He stands rigidly, his fists clenched. He might sit down or spring at* GUS *or weep.*

J.B. He couldn't think a thing like that. He . . .

He looks to DAVID *for reinforcement, but* DAVID *is standing there hurt and silent and self-horrified.* J.B. *goes to* DAVID.

Dave, you wouldn't want a thing like that. (*He shakes him.*) Dave!

DAVID (*glaring at* GUS). I'd cut my throat!

He walks downstage from J.B., *looking at* GUS. *His movements are wayward, restless, like one caught in a strange cul-de-sac.* GUS *is silent.*

Why do you look at me that way? (*Glances at* J.B. *then slowly back to* GUS.) Why do you look that way? I'm only telling you what happened. A person has to look at facts, doesn't he? I heard something at the door and I opened it . . . and there she was lying on the step. A fact is a fact, isn't it? (*They don't reply. Bursting out.*) Well, for Jesus sake, if you . . . !

GUS (*a shout*). What fact! She fell! So the baby is dead because she fell? Is this a fact?!!

DAVID (*moves away from* GUS's *direction, in high tension*). I didn't say dead. It doesn't have to be dead to be . . . to . . . (*Breaks off.*)

GUS. To be what?

Pause.

DAVID. To be a curse on us. It can come wrong . . . A fall can make them that way. The doctor told me. (GUS *looks unconvinced.*) The trouble with you is that you think I got a special angel watching over me.

SHORY (*pointing at* GUS). He said it that time, brother!

GUS (*to* SHORY *too*). A man needs a special angel to have a live child?

DAVID (*furiously*). Who said he was going to be dead?!

GUS. What are you excited about? (*Takes his arm.*) Take it easy, sit . . .

DAVID (*freeing his arm*). Stop humouring me, will you? Dan Dibble'll have my new mink here tonight. I got all the papers ready . . . (*Goes to a drawer, takes out papers.*) All you do is sign and . . .

GUS (*suddenly he rushes to David, pulls the papers out of his hand, throws them down*). Are you mad! (*He frightens* DAVID *into immobility.*) There is no catastrophe upstairs, there is no guarantee up there for your mink. (*He grasps* DAVID's *arm, pleadingly.*) Dave . . .

DAVID. If you say that again I'm going to throw you out of this house!

J.B. (*nervously*). Oh, come on now, come on now.

From above a scream of pain is heard. DAVID *freezes.* GUS *looks up.*

GUS (*to* DAVID). Don't say that again.

DAVID *thrusts his hands into his pockets as though they might reveal him too. Under great tension he attempts to speak reasonably. His voice leaps occasionally, he clears his throat.* GUS *never takes his eyes off him.* DAVID *walks from* J.B., *unwillingly.*

DAVID. I'm a lucky man, John. Everything I've ever gotten came . . . straight out of the blue. There's nothing mad about it. It's facts. When I couldn't have Hester unless Old man Falk got out of the way, he was killed just like it was specially for me. When I couldn't fix the Marmon . . . a man walks in from the middle of the night . . . and fixes it for me. I buy a lousy little gas station . . . they build a highway in front of it. That's lucky. You pay for that.

SHORY. Damn right you do.

GUS. Where is such a law?

DAVID. I don't know. (*Observes a silence. He walks to the windows.*) Of all the people I've heard of I'm the only one who's never paid. Well . . . I think the holiday's over. (*Turns towards upstairs, with great sorrow.*) I think we're about due to join up with the rest of you. I'll have almost sixty thousand dollars when I market my mink . . . but it won't be money I got without paying for it. And that's why I put everything in them. That's why I'm sure. Because from here on in we're paid for. I saw it in black and white when she fell. (*With a heartbroken tone.*) God help me, we're paid for now. I'm not afraid of my luck anymore, and I'm going to play it for everything it's worth.

GUS. David, you break my heart. This is from Europe this idea. This is from Asia, from the rotten places, not

America.

DAVID. No?

GUS. Here you are not a worm, a louse in the earth; here you are a man. A man deserves everything here!

SHORY. Since when?

GUS (*strongly to* SHORY). Since forever!

SHORY. Then I must have been born before that.

GUS (*angrily now*). I beg your pardon he is not you and do me a favour and stop trying to make him like you.

DAVID. He's not making me anything.

GUS. He won't be happy until he does, I can tell you! (*Indicating* SHORY.) This kind of people never are.

SHORY. What kind of people?

GUS. Your kind! *His* life he can make golden, if he wants.

SHORY. Unless the walls blow out.

GUS. If he don't go chasing after whores his walls won't blow out. (*Quietly.*) And I beg your pardon. I didn't mean nothing personal.

J.B. (*goes to* DAVID). I'll lend you the money for the mink, Dave.

GUS. Are you mad?

J.B. I can see what he means, Gus. (*Looks at* DAVE.) It takes a great kind of man to prepare himself that way. A man does have to pay. It's just the way it happens, senseless. (*He glances upstairs, then to* DAVE.)

It's true. It always happens senseless.

J.B. I'll back you, Dave.

DAVID. I'd like to pay him tonight if I can . . .

They all turn to look up as BELLE *appears, slowly descending the stairs. They do not hear her until she is a little way down. Her usual expression of wide-eyed bewilderment is on her face, but now she is tense, and descends looking at* DAVID. *She half sniffs, half sobs into her kerchief. She stops on the stairs.* DAVID *rises. She half laughs, half snivels in a quiet ecstasy of excitement, and weakly motions him upstairs. He comes toward her questioningly, to the landing.*

BELLE. Go . . . Go up.

DAVID. What. What . . . ?

BELLE (*suddenly bursts out and rushes down and flings her arms about him*). Oh, Davey, Davey.

DAVID (*ripping her free, he roars in her face*). What happened?! (*With a sob of grief in his voice, he grips her.*) Belle!

The cry of a baby is suddenly heard from above. The sound almost throws DAVID *back, away from the stairs. He stands stock still, hard as a rock, looking upward, his mouth fallen open.*

BELLE (*still half-sobbing*). It's a boy. A perfect baby boy!

She now breaks into full sobs and rushes up the stairs. Everything is still a moment, DAVID *stares at nothing. The cry sounds again. He looks upward again as though to let it sink in. J.B. goes to him, hand extended.*

J.B. (*filled with joy, and gravely*). DAVE.

DAVID dumbly shakes his hand, a weak smile on his face.

A boy, a boy, Dave! Just what you wanted!

A strange short laugh leaps from DAVID. *An easier but still tense laugh comes.* PAT *goes to him and shakes his hand.*

PAT. Dave, a new generation!

GUS (*smilingly*). Well? You see? (*Laughs.*) A good man gets what a good man makes. (*Hits* DAVID *jovially.*) Wake up now! Good luck!

Gus tosses a quarter to SHORY.

GUS. It's the first time you've been right since I knew you.

J.B. Come out of the ether. Take a look at her, Dave.

DAVID rushes out. They stand astonished for a moment.

What do you suppose come over him?

GUS. What else could come over him? . . . he's ashamed.

GUS *hurries out the door. The others remain in silence. Then one by one they look upstairs towards the sound of the baby's crying.*

Slow curtain.

Scene Two

Before the curtain rises thunder is heard.

It is one month later. The living room. Night.

The room is empty and in darkness. A bolt of lightning illuminates it through the windows, then darkness again. Now the door to the outside opens and HESTER *enters. She is very tense but her motions are minute, as though she were mentally absorbed and had entirely forgotten her surroundings. Without removing her coat or galoshes she comes to the centre of the room and stands there staring. Then she goes to a window and looks out. A flash of lightning makes her back a step from the window; and without further hesitation she goes to the phone, switching on a nearby light.*

HESTER (*she watches the window as she waits*). Hello? Gus? Where have you been, I've been ringing you for an hour. (*She listens.*) Well, look, could you come over here? Right now, I mean. It would *not* be interfering, Gus, I want to talk to you. He's outside. Gus, you've got to come here – his mink are going to die. (*She keeps glancing at the window.*) He doesn't know it yet, but he'll probably see it any minute. Dan Dibble called before . . . He's lost over thirty of his already . . . They use the same fish . . .

I want you here when he notices. (*She turns suddenly toward the door*.) He's coming in. You hurry over now . . . Please!

She hangs up, and starts for the door, but as though to compose herself she stops, and starts towards a chair when she realizes she still has her coat and galoshes on. She is kicking off the galoshes when DAVID *enters. He looks up at her, and with a slight glance upstairs . . .*

DAVID. Everything all right?

HESTER. Why?

DAVID. I thought I heard a call or a scream.

HESTER. No, there was no scream.

DAVID. I guess it was the lightning. Is he all right? (*Of the baby.*)

HESTER. There's no gate there, you can go up and see.

DAVID. How can I go to him with my hands so bloody? (*She turns from him. He starts for the door*)

HESTER. I thought you were through feeding.

DAVID. I am. I'm just grinding some for tomorrow.

HESTER. Are they all right?

DAVID. I never saw them so strung up. I think it's the hail banging on the cages. (*There is a momentary hiatus as he silently asks for leave to go.*) I just wondered if he was all right. (*He takes a step.*)

HESTER (*suddenly*). Don't go out again, Davey. Please. You told me yourself, they ought to be left alone when they're whelping.

DAVID. I've got to be there, Hess, I've just got to. I . . . (*He goes to her.*) I promise you, after they whelp we'll go away, we'll travel . . . I'm going to make a queen's life for you.

HESTER. Don't go out.

DAVID. I'll be in right away . . .

HESTER (*grasps his arms*). I don't want them to be so important, Davey!

DAVID. But everything we've got is in them. You know that.

HESTER. I'm not afraid of being poor . . .

DAVID. That's 'cause you never were – and you'll never be. You're going to have a life like a . . .

HESTER. Why do you keep saying that? I don't want it, I don't need it! I don't care what happens out there! And I don't want you to care. Do you hear what I say, I don't want you to care!

A bolt of lightning floods suddenly through the windows. DAVID *starts. Then hurries to the door.*

HESTER (*frightened now*). Davey! (DAVID *stops, does not turn.*) You can't stop the lightning, can you? (*He does not turn still. She goes closer to him, pleading.*) I know how hard you worked, but it won't be the first year's work that ever went for nothing in the world. It happens that way, doesn't it?

DAVID (*he turns to her slowly. Now his emotions seem to flood him*). Not when a man doesn't make any mistakes. I kept them alive all year. Not even one got sick. I didn't make a mistake. And now this storm comes, just when I need it calm, just tonight . . .

HESTER. You talk as though the sun were shining everywhere else but here, as though the sky is making thunder just to knock you down.

DAVID (*he looks at her long as though she had reached into him*). Yeh, that's the way I talk. (*He seems about to sob.*) Bear with me, Hess – only a little while. (*He moves to go.*)

HESTER. Davey . . . the house is grey. Like the old paint was creeping back on the walls. When will we sit and talk again? When will you pick up the baby . . . ?

DAVID (*comes alive*). I did, Hess . . .

HESTER. You never did. And why is that?

DAVID. When you were out of the house . . .

HESTER. Never, not since he's been born. Can't you tell me why? (DAVID *turns and opens the door. Her fear raises her voice.*) Can't you tell me why? (*He starts out.*) Davey, tell me why! (*He goes out. She calls out the door*) Davey, I don't understand! Come back here!

In a moment, she comes away, closing the door. Her hands are lightly clasped to her throat. She comes to a halt in the room; now she turns on another lamp. She suddenly hears something behind her, turns, and takes a step toward door as GUS *quietly enters.*

HESTER (*relieved*). Oh, Gus!

GUS (*glancing toward the door*). Is he coming right back?

HESTER. He goes in and out, I don't know. You'll stay here tonight, won't you?

GUS. The first thing to do is sit down.

As he leads her to the couch – she is near tears.

HESTER I kept calling you and calling you.

GUS (*taking off his coat*). Now get hold of yourself; there's nothing to do till he finds out. I'm sorry, I was in Burley all afternoon, I just got home. What did Dibble tell you? (*He returns to her.*)

HESTER. Just that he was losing animals, and he thought it was silkworm in the feed. They share the same carload.

GUS. Ah. David notices nothing? (*A gesture toward outside with his head.*)

HESTER. He just says they're strung up, but that's the lightning. It takes time for them to digest.

GUS. Well then, we'll wait and see. (*He goes to the window, looks out.*) This storm is going to wipe out the bridges. It's terrible.

HESTER. What am I going to do, Gus? He worked all year on those animals.

GUS. We will do what we have to, Hester, that's what we will do. (*He turns to her, taking out an envelope.*) Actually, I was coming over tonight anyway . . . To say goodbye.

HESTER. Goodbye!

GUS. In here I explain. (*He places the envelope on the mantel.*)

When I am gone, give it to him. I can't argue with him no more.

HESTER. You mean you're moving away?

GUS. I am going to Chicago. There is an excellent position for me. Double what I can make here.

HESTER. But why are you going?

GUS. I told you, I can make double . . .

HESTER (*gets up*). Don't treat me like a baby, why are you going? (*Slight pause.*)

GUS. Well . . . Actually, I am lonely. (*Laughs slightly.*) There is plenty of girls here, but no wifes, Hester. Thirty-seven years is a long time for a man to wash his own underwear.

HESTER (*touched*). You and your red-headed girls!

GUS. I was always a romantic man. You know that, don't you? Truly.

HESTER. But to give up a business and go traipsing off just for . . . ?

GUS. Why not? What made me give up Detroit to come here?

HESTER. Really, Gus?

GUS. Certainly. Moving is very necessary for me. (*Pause.*) I'm leaving tomorrow night.

HESTER. But why? I suppose I should understand, but I can't. (*Pause.* GUS *looks directly at her.*) It doesn't make sense. (*Insistently.*) Gus?

GUS (*pause. For a long time he keeps her in his eye*). Because I have no courage to stay here. (*Pause.*) I was talking today with a doctor in Burley. I believe David . . . is possibly losing his mind.

She does not react. She stands there gaping at him. He waits. With no sound she backs a few steps, then comes downstage and lightly sets both hands on the couch, never taking her eyes from him. A pause. As though hearing what he said again, she is impelled to move again, to a chair on whose back she sets a hand – facing him now. They stand so a moment.

I thought surely you knew. Or at least you would know soon. (*She does not answer.*) Do you know?

HESTER. I've almost thought so sometimes . . . But I can't believe he . . .

GUS (*a new directness, now that she has taken the blow*). I have been trying to straighten him out all month. But I have no more wisdom, Hester. I . . . I would like to take him to the doctors in Burley.

HESTER (*shocked*). Burley!

GUS. Tonight. They will know what to say to him there.

HESTER (*horrified*). No, he's not going there.

GUS. It is no disgrace. You are talking like a silly woman.

HESTER. He's not going there! There's nothing wrong with him. He's worried, that's all . . .

GUS. When those animals begin dying he will be more than worried. Nothing worse could possibly happen . . .

HESTER. No. If he can take the shock tonight he'll be all right. I think it's better if they die.

GUS. For God's sake, no!

HESTER. All his life he's been waiting for it. All his life, waiting, waiting for something to happen. It'll be over now, all over, don't you see? Just stay here tonight. And when it happens, you'll talk to him . . .

GUS. What he has lost I can't put back, Hester. He is not a piece of machinery.

HESTER (*stops moving*). What has he lost? What do you mean, lost?

GUS. What a man must have, what a man must believe. That on this earth he is the boss of his life. Not the leafs in the teacups, not the stars. In Europe I seen already millions of Davids walking around, millions. They gave up already to know that they are the boss. They gave up to know that they deserve this world. And now here too, with such good land, with such a . . . such a big sky they are saying . . . I hear it every day . . . that it is somehow unnatural for a man to have a sweet life and nice things.

Daily they wait for catastrophe. A man must understand the presence of God in his hands. And when he don't understand it he is trapped. David is trapped, Hester. You understand why everything he has is in the mink?

HESTER (*wide-eyed*). It's the baby, isn't it. He thought it was going to be . . .

GUS. Dead, yes. Say, say out now. I was here that night. He always wanted so much to have a son and that is why he saw him dead. This, what he wanted most of all he couldn't have. This finally would be his catastrophe. And then everything would be guaranteed for him. And that is why he put everything in those animals.

HESTER. Gus . . .

GUS. The healthy baby stole from David his catastrophe, Hester. Perfect he was born and David was left with every penny he owns in an animal that can die like this . . . (*Snaps his fingers.*) and the catastrophe still on its way.

HESTER (*seeing the reason*). He never touched the baby . . .

GUS. How can he touch him? He is bleeding with shame, Hester. Because he betrayed his son, and he betrayed you. And now if those animals die he will look into the tea leafs of his mind, into the sky he will look where he always looked, and if he sees retribution there . . . you will not call him worried any more. Let me take him to Burley before he notices anything wrong in the cages.

HESTER. No. He's Davey, he's not some . . .

GUS. They will know what to do there!

HESTER. I know what to do! (*She moves away and faces him.*) I could have warned him . . . Dan called before he started feeding.

GUS (*shocked and furious*). Hester!

HESTER. I wanted them dead! I want them dead now, those beautiful rats!

GUS. How could you do that!

HESTER. He's got to lose. Once and for all he's got to lose.

I always knew it had to happen, let it happen now, before
the baby can see and understand. You're not taking him
anywhere. He'll be happy again. It'll be over and he'll
be happy!

GUS (*unwillingly*). Hester.

HESTER. No, I'm not afraid now. It'll be over now.

GUS. What will be over, Hester? He took out last week an
insurance policy. A big one. (HESTER *stops moving.*) It
covers his life.

HESTER. No, Gus.

GUS. What will be over?

HESTER (*a cry*). No, Gus! (*Breaks into sobbing.*)

GUS (*taking her by the arms*). Get hold now, get hold!

HESTER (*sobbing, shaking her head negatively*). Davey,
Davey . . . he was always so fine, what happened to
him . . . !

GUS. He mustn't see you this way . . . ! Nothing is worse
than . . .

HESTER (*trying to break from GUS to go out*). Davey,
Davey . . . !

GUS. Stop it, Hester! He's shamed enough!

*He has her face in his hands as the door suddenly opens and
DAVID is standing there. GUS releases her. They stand apart.
DAVID has stopped moving in surprise. He looks at her, then
at GUS, then at her. DAVID goes toward her.*

DAVID (*astonished, alarmed*). Hess. What's the matter?

HESTER. Nothing . . . How is everything outside?

DAVID. It's still hailing . . . (*Stops. With an edge of self-
accusation.*) Why were you crying?

HESTER (*her voice still wet*). I wasn't really.

DAVID (*feeling the awkwardness, glances at both; to GUS*).
Why were you holding her?

HESTER (*with an attempt at a laugh*). He wasn't holding me.
He's decided to go to Chicago and . . .

DAVID (*mystified, to GUS*). Chicago! Why . . . ?

HESTER (*tries to laugh*). He wants to find a wife! Imagine?

DAVID (*to* GUS). All of a sudden you . . . ?

HESTER (*unbuttoning his coat, ready to weep and trying to be gay*). Let's have some tea and sit up till way late and talk! Don't go out any more, Davey . . . From now on I'm not letting you out of my sight . . . There are so many nice things to talk about!

She has his coat and has just stepped away with a gross animation.

DAVID (*deeply worried. Brushing her attempt away*). Why were you crying, Hester?

The phone rings. HESTER *fairly leaps at the sound. She starts quickly for the phone but* DAVID *is close to it and picks it up easily, slightly puzzled at her frantic eagerness to take it.*

HESTER. It's probably Ellie. I promised to lend her a hat for tomorrow.

DAVID (*looks at her perplexed. He lifts the receiver.*) Yes?

As he speaks HESTER *steps away from him in fear now.* GUS *changes position instinctively, almost as though for physical advantage.*

Mr Dibble? No, he isn't here; I don't expect him. Oh! Well, he isn't here yet. What's it all about? (*Listens.*) What are you talking about; have I got what under control? (*Listens. Now with horror.*) Of course I've fed! Why didn't you call me, you know I feed before this! God damn your soul, you know I use the same feed he does! (*Roars.*) Don't tell me he called me! Don't . . . ! (*Listens*) When did he call?

Breaks off; listens. He turns, listening, to HESTER; *slowly, an expression of horrified perplexity and astonishment grips his face. His eyes stay on* HESTER.

Well, they seem all right now . . . maybe it hasn't had

time to grip them. (*Still into the phone.*) Yeh . . . yeh . . . all right, I'll wait for him.

He hangs up weakly. For a long time he looks at her. Then he looks at GUS *and back to her as though connecting them somehow.*

What . . . Why . . . didn't you tell me he called?

HESTER (*suddenly she dares not be too near him; she holds out a hand to touch and ward him off . . . she is a distance from him*). Davey . . .

DAVID. Why didn't you stop me from feeding?

GUS. Dan'll be here. Maybe he can do something.

DAVID (*facing* HESTER). What can he do? Something's wrong in the feed! He can't pull it out of their stomachs! (*With welling grief. To* HESTER.) Why didn't you tell me? (HESTER *retreats a few inches.*) Why are you moving away from me? (*He suddenly reaches out and catches her arm.*) You wanted them to die!

HESTER (*straining at his grip*). You always said something had to happen. It's better this way, isn't it?

DAVID. Better?! My boy is a pauper, we're on the bottom of a hole, how is it better!

HESTER (*her fear alone makes her brave*). Then I . . . I think I'll have to go away, Davey. I can't stay here, then.

She moves toward the stairs. He lets her move a few steps, then moves across to her and she stops and faces him.

DAVID. You can't . . . What did you say?

HESTER. I can't live with you, Davey. Not with the baby.

DAVID. No, Hester . . .

HESTER. I don't want him to see you this way. It's a harmful thing. I'm going away.

DAVID (*he breathes as though about to burst into weeping. He looks to* GUS, *stares at him, then back to her. Incredibly*). You're going with him?

HESTER (*she darts a suddenly frightened glance toward* GUS).
Oh, no, no, I didn't mean that. He was going anyway.

DAVID (*it is truer to him now*). You're going with him.

HESTER. No, David, I'm not going with anybody . . .

DAVID (*with certainty. Anger suddenly stalks him*). You're
going with him!

HESTER. No, Davey . . . !

DAVID (*To* GUS). You told her not to tell me!

HESTER. He wasn't even here when Dan phoned!

DAVID. How do I know where he was! (*To* GUS) You think
I'm a blind boy?!

HESTER. You're talking like a fool!

DAVID. You couldn't have done this to me! He wants you!

He starts to stride for GUS. HESTER *gets in front of him.*

HESTER. I did it! (*Grabs his coat.*) Davey, I did it myself!

DAVID. No, you couldn't have! Not you! (*To* GUS.) You
think I've fallen apart? You want her . . . ?

He starts to push her aside, knocking a chair over, going for
GUS. *She slaps him hard across the face. He stops moving.*

HESTER (*with loathing and heartbreak*). I did it!

*For an instant they are still, she watching for his reaction. He
quietly draws in a sob, looking at her in grief.*

HESTER. I wanted you like you were, Davey – a good man,
able to do anything. You were always a good man, why
can't you understand that?

DAVID. A good man! You pick up a phone and everything
you've got dies in the ground! A man! What good is a
man!

HESTER. You can start again, start fresh and clean!

DAVID. For what! For what!! The world is a madhouse,
what can you build in a madhouse that won't be knocked
down when you turn your back!

HESTER. It was you made it all and you destroyed it! I'm

going, Davey . . . (*With a sob.*) I can't bear any more. (*She rushes to the landing.*)

DAVID (*A call, and yet strangled by sobs*). Hester . . .

HESTER *halts, looks at him. His hands raised towards her, shaken and weeping, he moves toward the landing . . . frantically.*

I love you . . . I love you . . . Don't . . . don't . . . don't.

He reaches her, and sobbing, lost, starts drawing her down to him as the door, left, swings open. DAN DIBBLE *rushes in and halts when he sees* DAVID. *He carries a small satchel.*

DIBBLE (*indicating downstage, right*). I've been out there looking for you, what are you doing in here? I've got something may help them. Come on. (*He starts for the door.*)

DAVID. I don't want to look at them, Dan. (*He goes to a chair.*)

DIBBLE. You can't be sure, it might take . . . (*Opens the door.*)

DAVID. No, I'm sure they digested, it's over two hours.

DIBBLE (*stops moving suddenly at door*). Over two hours what?

DAVID. Since I fed them.

DIBBLE. You didn't give them this morning's load of fish?

DAVID. What else could I give them? The load I split with you, goddamit.

DIBBLE. Well, you just couldn't've, David. They don't show a sign yet: that kind of silkworm'll kill them in twenty minutes. You must've . . .

DAVID. Silkworm. – But my fish wasn't wormy . . .

DIBBLE. They don't look like worms, they're very small, you wouldn't have noticed them, they're black, about the size of a . . .

DAVID. Poppyseed . . .

DIBBLE. A grain of ground pepper, yah. Come on . . . (*But*

DAVID *is motionless, staring . . .*) Well? You want me to look at them?

DAVID *slowly sits in a chair.*

GUS. At least have a look, Dave. (*Slight pause.*)

DAVID. (*wondrously; but also an edge of apology*). . . . I saw them, Dan. I didn't know what they were but I decided not to take any chances, so I threw them away.

DIBBLE (*angering*). But you couldn't have gone over every piece of fish!

DAVID. Well I . . . yah, I did, Dan. Most of it was okay, but the ones with the black specks I threw away.

HESTER. Davey! – you saved them!

DAVID. Well, you told me to watch the feed very carefully, Dan – I figured you'd notice them the same as me!

DIBBLE. But you know nobody's got the time to go over every goddam piece of fish!

DAVID. But I thought everybody did! – I swear, Dan!

DIBBLE. God Almighty, Dave, a man'd think you'd warn him if you saw silkworm! – the least you could've done is call me.

DAVID. I started to, I had the phone in my hand – but it seemed ridiculous, me telling you something. Listen, let me give you some of my breeders to start you off again.

DIBBLE. No – no . . .

DAVID. Please, Dan, go out and pick whatever you like.

DIBBLE. . . . Well, I might think about that, but I'm too old to start all over again, I don't think I could get up the steam. Well, goodnight.

DIBBLE *exits.*

GUS *and* HESTER *stand watching* DAVID *who is puzzled and astonished.*

DAVID. I can't believe it. He's the best in the business.
GUS. Not any more.

HESTER. This wasn't something from the sky, dear. This was you only. You must see that now, don't you?

The baby crying is heard from above.

I'd better go up, he's hungry. Come up? – Why don't you, Dave?

DAVID (*awkwardly*).

I will . . . right away.

(HESTER *exits. His face is rapt.*) But they couldn't all have made their own luck! – J.B. with his drinking, Shory with his whores, Dad and Amos . . . and you losing your shop. (*Seizing on it.*) And I could never have fixed that Marmon if you hadn't walked in like some kind of an angel! – that Marmon wasn't me!

GUS. You'd have towed it to Newton and fixed it there without me. (*Grasps* DAVID'*s hand.*) But is that really the question anyway? Of course bad things must happen. And you can't help it when God drops the other shoe. But whether you lay there or get up again – that's the part that's entirely up to you, that's for sure.

DAVID. You don't understand it either, do you.

GUS. No, but I live with it. All I know is you are a good man, but also you have luck. So you have to grin and bear it – you are lucky!

DAVID. For now.

GUS. Well, listen – 'for now' is a very big piece of 'forever'.

HESTER (*from above*). Dave? You coming up?

GUS. Go on, kiss the little fellow.

DAVID. . . . I had the phone in my hand to call him. And I put it down. I had his whole ranch right here in my hand.

GUS. You mean you were a little bit like God . . . for him.

DAVID. Yes. Except I didn't know it.

GUS (*a thumb pointing heavenward*). Maybe he doesn't know either.

HESTER (*from above*). David? Are you there?

GUS. Goodnight, Dave.

DAVID (*with a farewell wave to* GUS, *calls upstairs*). Yes, I'm here!

He goes to the stairs. A shock of thunder strikes. He quickly turns toward the windows, the old apprehension in his face.

. . . (*To himself.*) For now.
(*With a self-energized determination in his voice and body.*) Comin' up!

As he mounts the stairs a rumble of thunder sounds in the distance.

Afterword

The two plays in this volume were both written in the early 1940s. One was produced (running for four days); one was not. They were not Arthur Miller's first. If we think of his public career as commencing in 1947, with the success of *All My Sons*, we have to go back more than a decade to find its true beginning. He wrote his first play, *No Villain*, in the middle of the Depression, while a second year student at the University of Michigan. There followed a series of works in which he tested his skills and explored his response to private and public issues. Nor were all of them simply five-finger exercises. Two won drama prizes: *They Too Arise* was even produced, though in a place and at a time when it was hardly likely to attract attention. Even *Honors at Dawn* and *The Great Disobedience*, (also creations of his Michigan years and more obviously apprentice work), compare not unfavourably with the products of a theatre whose own melodrama frequently matched that of the period.

These were plays which expressed the vaguely held beliefs of a writer trying to make sense of the economic crisis which had come close to ruining his own family and which had challenged the most fundamental myths and basic political and social conventions of a nation. Interestingly, they bear the imprint of his Jewish identity as none of his published plays were to do until the 1960s. The rhetoric clearly lacks the control of his later work, a control that he was often to achieve through writing first in verse and then in prose. In these plays meaning undeniably bubbles too freely to the surface. He frequently discharges in words what he would later be content to express through character and action. There is also plainly a good deal more than a whiff of melodrama. But a starkly Manichean decade generated its own necessities and urgencies and he simply responded to those pressures in common with others who were joining in a national debate about the meaning and direction of American society.

Having left university, and after a brief experience of unemployment, Miller joined the Federal Theatre, writing a comedy called *Listen My Children*, with a fellow Michigan student, Norman Rosten. It was never produced and by mid-1939 the Federal Theatre itself was dead, killed by an act of Congress. Though he did eventually get work on radio, writing brief plays for the Columbia Workshop and the Cavalcade of America, his immediate future lay in truck-driving and work as a shipfitter in the Brooklyn Navy Yard. But he did not stop writing and in 1939 he began another play, quite the most accomplished of his early dramas, *The Golden Years*. He completed this in 1940; the typescript bears his Brooklyn address, 1350 East Third Street.

With the sudden collapse of the Federal Theatre he decided to send the play to the Theatre Guild who promptly lost it. It finally emerged some years later, discovered in a discarded file. I came across it forty years later, still in the Miller archives at the University of Texas and persuaded the BBC to broadcast it on national radio. This was the first and so far only production of a play whose originality and language finally prompted enthusiastic reviews nearly fifty years after Miller sat down to write it in the first year of the Second World War.

The Golden Years is an assured piece of work. A contemplation of history, a character study, a drama of conflicting myths and values, it stands out from Miller's other plays of the 1930s in its language and in its subtlety of thought and action. To be sure, the debate between Montezuma and Cortez, which lies at its heart, is in a sense a continuation of that conflict between material and spiritual values which had characterized everything he had written up to that time and, indeed, was to continue to write. In that sense, at least, he has always been close kin to Eugene O'Neill, who saw his own essential theme as being embodied in the question: what shall it profit a man if he inherit the whole world and lose his soul? Until now, however, that opposition had been conceived largely in political terms, with a corrupt capitalism exerting its rights over those who found themselves its alienated products. In this play both men are the victims of their own systems of thought.

Cortez comes in search of gold and men's souls. The one will give him material wealth, the other, a more profound sense of conquest. He thrills to the sense of power which he derives from the Aztec confusion over his status as returned god or conquering general, no less than from the mere fact of his victories. But Montezuma, too, sees himself as a potential deity, for if Cortez is indeed one of the gods then his own life glows with significance and he is assimilated to the divinity which he is tempted to acknowledge in the Spanish conqueror. He becomes the apogee of Aztec historical, moral and metaphysical development.

Though one man is fated to be the conqueror and the other the conquered, there is an irony which goes beyond the defeat of a large and powerful people by a handful of adventurers. While Cortez appears little more than a cunning military leader drawn on by a lust for wealth and power, there is plainly something more to him, something detected by the Aztec woman, Marina, who defects to him, and by Montezuma, who defers to him. To a large degree the meaning they see in the invader is the meaning which they project upon him, but there is a quality in the man which commands attention from those who oppose him as well as from his own troops, though this element in his character, not elaborated by Miller, never threatens to disable him.

Montezuma, however, is disabled, caught in an irony of his own making. He stays his hand against Cortez not simply because he sees in him a man who may be a returned god, but because he now distrusts the violence on which his own empire has been built. Cortez oversees the destruction of the patterned grace of the Aztec city as he does the rendering down of gold ornaments and religious objects into crude ingots. In doing so he refuses to acknowledge a meaning to the lives he takes; he nullifies their beliefs, destroys their history and denies their art. He is the barbarian glorifying in the destruction of the work of finer minds and sensibilities. In some senses, indeed, his very absoluteness constitutes part of his fascination. But neither Montezuma nor Marina can bring themselves to believe that such implacability exists. They look for something else and in looking partly convince themselves that they have found it. They search for this quality because they are looking for some validation of the logic of their own lives. Themselves exhausted by a lifetime of cruelty and violence they look for some sanction for their own abandonment of it. Marina responds to the Christian message of love, failing to decode it in terms of the imperial ambition and simple venality that it cloaks. Montezuma projects onto Cortez the symbols of Aztec mythology, allegorizing as reborn hope what is in fact the extinction of that hope. They are both the victims not only of Cortez but of their own inability to decipher the code of experience, to understand the fatally flawed character of human nature.

In part this is a play inspired by and addressing a contemporary situation. Throughout Miller's early work there are references to his awareness of events in Europe, and in particular the threat to the Jews. He had seen Hitler's demands met not by united resistance but by equivocation. The desire for peace had led to a policy of appeasement, of which Munich in 1938 had merely been the formal codification. It was as though Europe was mesmerized by the power which confronted it, as though the very implacable nature of that power inspired a mixture of fascination and submissiveness. In that sense the play seems to be offered as an attempt to understand that process. The shadow which creeps across the moon in the opening scene, an eclipse whose meaning the Aztecs struggle to understand, offering up a sacrifice in the hope that this will clarify meaning as well as appease the gods, is not without its political import. As Montezuma observes of himself, learning his lesson too late:

> . . . while his eyes were heavenward in search of meaning and signs, a sword was pointing at his breast, and as it caught the light with such brilliant glare, it seemed to hold the sanction of the sun, and he dared not turn the killing blade away. And when the sun was set, and the light was gone, the emperor felt for the face of the god that he hoped would be there in the sword; but the time was late, and the sun was gone, and the steel stood turning in his heart.

But, as that speech makes plain, beyond the level of political allegory there is a concern, on the part of both Montezuma and Cortez, to emblematize the world, to read the meaning of experience.

Montezuma looks for signs and portents; Cortez sees the shape of his own identity as emerging from his Mexican adventures. The world is a text to be translated and hence re-written by those with the will and the power to do so. But there is a degree of wilfulness to this that enables other interpretations to be missed. Lacking the key to the cipher both men fail to grasp what it is they sacrifice and destroy and in whose name they render up their real grasp on immortality. They collude in the undermining of their joint ambition: Cortez is left holding nothing more than gold and Montezuma the fragments of an empire broken by a mere man. Both turn out to be less than they would have wished as the meaning they sought dissolves into simple anarchy. The imagination's power to make the world dissolves in the face of egotism and ambition. It is not simply that the poetic sensibility of Montezuma is shattered by the prosaic Cortez but that the effort to see a presiding will behind the hieroglyphs of experience, to read coherence into the sheer contingency of event, collapses, not least because of the hubris which that effort at translation implies. The universe must be made to mean, to contain a cipher, so that the self which observes it can thereby claim significance.

Montezuma employs his priests and metaphysicians to perform this task; Cortez his troops. The one now relies on words, the other on action, but they become locked together in a futile wrestling match, two sides of a warring personality in which both are losers. Montezuma has exhausted the power of conquest to render up the meaning which he seeks; Cortez still clings to it. He comes, as he claims, to bring the Word, to impose a system of belief and meaning which will trade salvation for gold. He leaves with no dignity, no souls in his care and only such gold as he can snatch away to try to buy himself back into the good favour of his king. The looked-for conversion of the Aztecs is denied him and hence the thing which would have enabled him to see himself as something other than a pirate, a plunderer of wealth. The Word is denied by action. Language is revealed as deceit. Meaning itself is threatened. God is mocked.

Both the play's protagonists are victims of their own language. They become what they speak. Certainly, Montezuma chooses to deflect into words what he might more logically and necessarily express through action. Cortez is drawn on by his own soldier's vocabulary. Lacking the imagination to understand what he is being offered, failing to read the meaning of the world which he encounters, he derives his sense of coherence from process, from action itself. He is in love with strategy, with the moment. Time is his enemy and as a result he never pauses to ask himself the meaning of actions which seem to carry their own apparent justification.

Not the least significant consequence of this emphasis on language is the extent to which the play generates a suspicion of its own rhetoric. It does contain overheated prose which production might have modified (and which Miller did slightly modify for the radio version) but as bombast is a natural resort for Cortez so the metaphors of Montezuma reveal his desire to deny the actual, the real, the immediate in the name of the desired, the metaphysical, the potential. He seeks refuge in ambivalence and opacity. His language removes him from contact with the tangible world just as taboos deny him physical contact with the people. Metaphor reconciles the irreconcilable. He is a poet. He has the poet's pride that he can force opposites to co-exist, that he can create in words what does not exist in nature. He rides the tiger of his words and realizes too late that he has destroyed himself by his pretension. Now, belatedly, he feels the poet's incapacity before a brute reality, as Auden was to confess his own poetry's inability to save a single Jew from the gas chambers. And yet, of course, that incapacity is modified by Miller's own refusal to be silenced by the paradox. His metaphor survives the irony as Montezuma's does not. The very historical perspective ironizes the idea of the golden years to which the Aztec king sacrificed his kingdom. We read his actions through our knowledge of his fate and it is that knowledge which destabilizes the symbol to which he is drawn and which negates the stance which he adopts.

Miller's play, of course, is no less a metaphor and he, too, could be accused of placing altogether too much faith in its magic, but it is the condition of his craft. He knows that even the writer who urges a distrust of writing – Whitman no less than Beckett – is in thrall to the irony he would urge us to transcend. That ambiguity exists equally in the necessary act of resistance which the play seems to urge, in so far as it may involve the surrender of the values in whose name it will be initiated. But that, too, is an irony which has to be sustained. To resist Cortez, Montezuma has to become Cortez or at least to retreat to his own former violence; in other words he must take a step back down the evolutionary path and the sense of loss which that fact implies is the subject of the play, even as the fact of the play's own inadequacy to its task is a confession that the visions of art have no more redeemed men than the visions of priests.

The Golden Years catches a world on the turn. Montezuma is in thrall to the past. It literally freezes him into inaction. Cortez severs his ties to the past. He has no respect for or understanding of tradition. Montezuma is an expression of history and its agent: Cortez sees himself as its maker. The debate is a real one. Just as Tennessee Williams, in *A Streetcar Named Desire*, was to be attracted and repelled by both Blanche Dubois and Stanley Kowalski – the one representing a cultured but corrupt past, the other a vital but brutal future – so Miller acknowledges the countervailing strengths and weaknesses of his two protagonists. In some respects, too, their differing stances are not unrelated to his sense of an American society which he had already represented as being in transition, but here the balance is finer than, for example, it had been in *Honors at Dawn*. Innocence is no longer balanced, as it was in that play, against a cynical corruption. Montezuma's own hands are stained with blood. His own empire was founded on force; he has simply exhausted the possibilities of that avenue to meaning.

It is, however, the element of doubt that has entered Montezuma's world which constitutes his claim on our attention. Politically and historically his significance lies in his role as a defender of existing order, as a bastion against a new technological barbarism. Morally, his fascination lies in his sudden awareness of an ambiguity which is not wholly an escape from the pressure of immediate reality. In search of the absolute he has stumbled on doubt and eventually on guilt and even, for a few redemptive moments at the end of his life, on responsibility. What could have been simply the obliteration of a culture and the annihilation of a self-deceived individual becomes something more. Meaning, it appears, can be snatched from defeat and since that is also a vital element of tragedy perhaps what we are seeing here is the beginning of that flirtation with tragedy which was to lead Miller, a few decades later, to elaborate his ideas on modern tragedy and lay claims for Willy Loman as a tragic hero. There is, in fact, a self-consciously Shakespearian ring to Montezuma's enumeration of the natural disasters and portents which seem to be harbingers of Cortez and indications that something is rotten in the state of Mexico ('the world is . . . profligate with signs that point to some cancer in the heart of the state'), as there is in the connection which he makes between civil disturbance and metaphysi-

Both Montezuma and Cortez seem to believe that meaning is derived from the suffering of others, necessary sacrifices for the good of the state. In the case of Cortez the irony is sharper since he brings news of Christ's love, a truth to be imposed by the sword. But there is an irony, too, for Montezuma, as his own dream of a world without violence, without the violence, indeed, in which he had collaborated, is destroyed by a man who preaches the brotherhood of man and the god of peace: 'I saw another world,' laments Montezuma, 'a world where every door stood wide unbolted in the night, where the single ear of corn grew heavy as a child, and all the brass of war, swords and shields, were melted into rivers and the silver sea. Let a dream depart as it came . . . into the sunrise . . . I cannot bring my hand to kill it yet.' It is that refusal to allow a dream to slip away which precipitates his destruction.

Miller was not the only playwright to debate this issue at this time, nor the only one to imply that pacifism was no longer an appropriate response in the context of a world confronted by brutal power. The situation in Europe, which plainly lies behind this confrontation between an Aztec king and his callous invader, forced more than one American playwright to see this as creating a new set of necessities often at odds with their own earlier convictions. Nor was Miller the only writer to seek out an historical analogy. In *Abe Lincoln in Illinois* Robert Sherwood abandoned his earlier pose of cynical detachment for an insistence on the need for action. Abe Lincoln is shown relinquishing his pacifism in the face of a challenge to fundamental freedom. As he insists, 'Perhaps we have come to the dreadful day of awakening and the dream is ended'. In *Idiot's Delight* (1936) Sherwood had seen war as an extension of exploitation, with man turned against man for the benefit of industrialists and politicians. In *There Shall Be No Night* (1940), that changes as a pacifist scientist comes to understand the necessity for resistance. Maxwell Anderson similarly abandoned his pacifism and in *Key Largo* (1939) rejected his own earlier self-doubts as he exposed the cynicism which seemed to have fostered appeasement. It was time, he suggested, for commitment.

> . . . now that the sky's found empty
> a man has to be his own god for himself –
> has to prove to himself that a man can die
> for what he believes – if ever the time comes to him
> when he's asked to choose.

Just such a conviction is finally felt by Montezuma who comes at last to feel that his fate lies in his own hands and not in those of a god. In Maxwell Anderson's earlier play, *Winterset* (1935), that realisation, along with the conviction that anguished attempts to decipher the code of experience lead nowhere but to despair, becomes the basis of his own sense of the distinction between the tragic and the absurd:

this is the glory of earth-born men and women,
not to cringe, never to yield, but standing,
take defeat implacable and defiant,
die unsubmitting . . .
                         On this star
in this hard star-adventure, knowing not . . .
what the fires mean to right and left, nor whether
a meaning was intended or presumed,
men can stand up, and look out blind, and say:
in all these turning lights I find no clue,
only a masterless night, and in my blood
no certain answer, yet is my mind my own.

Something of the same kind seems implied by Montezuma ('while his eyes were heavenward in search of meanings and signs, a sword was pointed at his breast') and the play's ending celebrates not merely the spirit of resistance implied by his own death at the hands of his people, as he comes to represent the oppression against which they finally rebel, but also, perhaps, another freedom as they learn to construct the meaning of their own lives independently of their gods and of the king who is their gods' representative.

By one of those curious coincidences another play making essentially the same analogy was transmitted by NBC radio in their series 'Lands of the Free' in July 1943, by which time Miller's own text was already completed. Written by Morton Wishengrad, former director of the AFL (American Federation of Labor) Shortwave Bureau, where he worked as a speech writer for labour leaders, it deals with the relationship between the Spanish and the Incas. Like Miller, Wishengrad wrote scripts for 'Cavalcade of America' and *The Lost Inca* was eventually published in 1947 in the same volume of radio plays which included Miller's own *The Story of Gus*. What is significant is less the play than the analogy which it offered to the situation in Europe – an analogy spelt out by the book's editor, Joseph Liss:

Here is a play of purpose out of yesterday's history that tells us that yesterday's tyrants are the blood-and-money brothers of today's tyrants. If this drama were a mirror in Hell, Hitler and his cronies would see that their murderous deeds were not original. They would see themselves and other cruelties reflected in the image of the Corregidors and the Viceroys of sixteenth century Spain who came to exploit the Incas . . . Even the cruelties are somewhat similar: the Spaniards burned out the tongues of rebellious Indians; the Nazis burned the whole body. And the purpose of these men and their governments? The same too. Slavery of the weak for markets and gold to give the tyrant strength to get more markets and more gold. Cruelty has a purpose.

When Tupac, the last Inca prince, cries out 'I should have died resisting. Indians of Peru. I have betrayed you. I have been used by the Spaniards. I have been a traitor', he is making a confession very like that made by Montezuma in Miller's play. Both men do finally resist and die in doing so and it is clear that this necessity is a central thrust in both plays. But *The Golden Years* is a work which does far more than offer an historical analogy for a contemporary evil, – which is why it could still be produced with effect in 1987.

In 1939 the President of the Dramatists' Guild, Robert Sherwood, converted now to the need for united action in defence of liberty, called on writers to lend their talents to the war against Hitler. 'Words which may originate in the mind of someone here in this room,' he insisted, when addressing a meeting of playwrights, 'may be brought to people of all kinds and kindreds who are hungry for them – who may be stimulated by them to a new faith in the brotherhood of life – who may, for all any of us can tell, be saved by them.' Perhaps Miller was responding to this and other calls with *The Golden Years* but if so it amounts to much more than an invitation to brotherhood. The first play he had written which in its subject was completely remote from his experience, it is also the first of his works in which control of character, plot and language seem close to that which he was to evidence in his Broadway successes a few years later. As *Times* reviewer Peter Davalle remarked, in his November 1987 review: 'this early Miller has flashes of insight (and certainly of poetry) that are worthy to stand alongside anything in later Miller. His chronicle about the confrontation between . . . Montezuma and . . . Cortez inevitably calls to mind Peter Shaffer's *The Royal Hunt of the Sun* . . . Put the two plays side by side, try to forget the breath-taking staging of Shaffer's play, and Miller has the edge on the competition.'

The first of Miller's plays to receive a professional production, *The Man Who Had All The Luck* opened on 23rd November, 1944, and closed four days later. Its only publication was in a wartime collection, long since out of print. Seldom produced (its first London staging took place sixteen years after its New York première), it is not without its flaws but, coming as it did three years before his first public success, it reveals a writer already resistant to the apparent realism of his own settings, already intent on welding the psychological to the social, the political and the metaphysical, already concerned to press character to the point at which it threatens to fracture.

The Man Who Had All The Luck is clearly a work that fascinates Arthur Miller. Well over forty years after its first production he was still revising it, still debating with himself the appropriateness of its ending. Indeed even the original play was itself a reworking of an earlier three hundred and sixty page novel (begun in 1941 and never published), which moved its protagonist from healthy ambition to insanity, from a life-centred energy force to death. The play which he derived from this and which was copyrighted in 1943, together with a further revision which was the basis for a production in 1944, settled for a gentler version in which redemption is available and irony succumbs to love. He was never entirely happy with this. Indeed, in an interview in the 1980s he revealed that he was contemplating revising the play so that it would come into line with the novel's ending, feeling that, in some ways, this was the more logical outcome of a story in which self-doubt intensified to the point of self-annihilation (thereby, incidentally, bringing it into line with the true story on which it was based). After all, did not all of his plays – from *The Golden Years* (1943) until *A View from the Bridge* (1955) – end in the death of the protagonist as the final meaning of a life was forced to offer itself up at the moment of death? In the event, when he did modify the play, for a staged reading in 1988, he reprieved his protagonist from the death sentence he had been tempted to pronounce.

The novel, based in part on the experiences of his first wife's aunt, tells the story of David Frieber, whose success as an auto-mechanic quickly leads to success in a number of other fields. Even his private life gives him everything he could have desired. Though his marriage to Hester had been opposed by her bigoted parents she had broken free with no difficulty so that the father's subsequent death removed an irritant rather than an obstacle. In time they have the child for which they long; everything, indeed, seems to fall into their hands.

By contrast, they are surrounded by people whose lives have failed to blossom. There is Gus, a German mechanic whose own auto-repair business unaccountably founders, and Shory, a double amputee who had lost his legs in the war. Most painfully, there is J.B. Feller, a reformed alcoholic, who inadvertently suffocates the child on which he and his wife dote, in a scene which prefigures that in Joseph Heller's *Something Happened*. And, in what is the most extended sub-plot of the novel, Patterson Beeves, who has trained his son for a career in baseball practising in the basement through the close seasons, discovers that his obsessive training has in fact unfitted the boy for major league competition. For David Frieber, this very contrast is at the root of an anxiety that deepens into despair and finally madness as he tries to make sense of their failure and his own success.

He wishes to believe in a natural order in which he can locate himself. He needs to feel that there is such a thing as justice. When he expresses doubts about his own acquired skills as a mechanic it is because he suspects 'he was improvising where he should have been following engineering procedure.' For if there is no governing principle, no moral equilibrium to be sustained, then all things are possible. With no God in heaven (and religion, in the novel, has a baleful influence), he is left with nothing more elevated that the pure arbitrariness of experience. So, in apparent contradiction to his earlier remark, he argues strenuously that 'some people think that things just happen to them, and things just push them along. That's wrong. People *make* things happen to themselves. A person can make anything happen if he wants to badly enough . . . You can make yourself whatever you want to. It's the person that makes things happen . . . Whatever he wants, mind you – money, fame, fortune.' This apparently confident statement, however, comes less out of conviction than a nervous self-doubt which intensifies as the novel progresses, while the reference to 'money, fame, fortune' suggests the extent to which he is echoing a national myth rather than defining a personal faith. Indeed he comes to feel that life is 'without dignity . . . without sense' unless it can be redeemed by the birth of a child who will make you 'a part of the universe.' So, he longs for a child 'as a meaning in his life.' He is rewarded but when he sees J.B's child killed in an ironic accident (the drunken father inadvertently smothers the baby when he tosses pillows onto the bed where it is sleeping), this logic is broken. Now he comes to feel that 'there is no accounting for his life, it was not under his control, neither his fortunes nor his fate.' Besides, how do you judge success except by the relative failure of others? David becomes aware of the complicity which this implies as he learns of the unaccountable failure of his friend Gus, confessing 'I have wished it somewhere hidden in my blood.' This was a theme, not developed here, to which he would return more than twenty years later in *After the Fall*.

The echoes of Miller's college Marxism present in his early plays are still to be heard here – though more so in the novel than in the play. Thus, on one level, David's is a classic case of alienation, helpfully diagnosed by a European working man, Gus:

> A man must see what he makes with his hands, it is not enough to make money . . . A man must see every day what he has done by the moving of his hands, the things that he makes. There is nothing the matter with you, David. With you is only the same as with millions of people, they are not living so that they are allowed to see what comes from their hands.

At root this was to be Willy Loman's problem in *Death of a Salesman*. He, too, would wish to leave his mark on the world, to define himself through what he creates. He is never so much himself as when he is working with his hands. But that, of course, is not what he does, for, as a salesman, he makes nothing, having only himself to sell.

But in neither case was Miller content to offer solely a social analysis. Willy is pressed in the direction of psychosis and David to the point of literal insanity by what they perceive as the absurdity of their lives unless redeemed. For Willy that redemption lies through love, albeit a love imperfectly perceived and incapable of deflecting him from his illusions. For David, in the novel, there is no redemption, real or imagined, as absurdity becomes a threatening force draining individual will of meaning. Gus may insist (unconsciously echoing David's own earlier remarks) that it 'Is only hands behind the palaces, hands behind the kings, hands behind everything, the worst and the best, the good and bad . . . Nothing is in the sky . . . Everything comes only from your hands,' but David, by the end of the novel, is unable to accept this account of life. For Gus, the problem is essentially a social one as, unable to see the products of their labour, people forget 'that everything is from the hands.' For David, the problem is more fundamental and he falls to his death from a nearby cliff, embracing the absurdity whose reality he has come to accept.

The original play version, which was published in 1944 before it was staged, in a collection of new American writing called *Cross-Section*, edited by Edwin Seaver, differs from the novel in a number of crucial respects. In particular, David Frieber's rise now becomes more precipitate and apparently more dependent on fate. In contrast to the novel, his career is here launched by the sheer chance of a competent mechanic (Gus) appearing on the scene at a crucial moment (as he is challenged to repair the car of an influential local farmer). In the novel he merely subcontracts the job in question to a nearby garage and later, jokingly, admits as much. In the novel, Hester's father is dead and his objections to her marrying David had anyway carried little weight with the couple. In the play, he is still alive and vehement in his opposition, an opposition to which Hester somewhat mysteriously acquiesces, until his sudden and unexpected death removes a real obstacle to their happiness. Later, Frieber's service station dramatically increases in value when a new highway is constructed.

The play, in other words, turns on a series of coincidences which seem painfully contrived, but their arbitrariness, their ironies, constitute precisely the challenge that David Frieber has to confront. For the world which rewards him punishes those around him. David becomes a mirror image of Job. Where Job has to make sense of his ill-fortune and, finally, to submit to a will whose logic he will never penetrate, David tries to make sense of his good fortune until, finally, he has to acknowledge his power to intervene in his own life. Where in the novel he surrenders to absurdity, here he acts, or is persuaded to act, in such a way as to deny it its power. Where in the novel he dies, in the play he survives, saved by his wife's common sense no less than her love.

David is surrounded by those who believe in fate, in inevitability. There is Patterson (Pat) Beeves, whose desire to secure a place in major league baseball for his son, Amos, does not extend to contacting the clubs, because 'I always thought of it happening . . . naturally . . . just happen.' His aunt Belle, a minor character, has deferred her life, never quite getting around to assuming responsibility for her own actions. If she seems a caricature this is, partly at least, an expression of her failure to create her own identity. Like Patterson Beeves, like the cynical store owner, Shory, she lives vicariously. And it is Shory, modelled, perhaps, in part, on the figure of Moe Axelrod in Clifford Odets' *Awake and Sing*, who is given the clearest statement of the metaphysical absurdity against which the play rebels. A man who had lost his legs in an accident at the very end of a war to whose dangers he had considered himself immune, he is convinced that, 'A man is a jellyfish laying on the beach. A wave comes along and pulls him back into the sea, and he floats a while on a million currents he can't even feel, and he's back on the beach again never knowing why.'

In this, the first play version, David himself is a fatalist. When a rival mechanic comes into town he accepts that this is 'just the way it ought to be, the way it . . . happened.' His own career is one he 'just fell into . . . by accident.' But where Shory sees this as evidence of sheer contingency, David has to believe in some underlying principle of justice: 'If people don't receive according to what they deserve inside them we're living in a madhouse.' The apparently unjustified failure of his friends, however, lends an increasing air of desperation to his declarations of faith in a coherent universe. 'People,' he insists, 'get what they deserve . . . You end up with what you deserve inside . . . Otherwise anything can happen . . . anything at any time! The most terrible things . . . There's no use living if . . . There must be a reason for these things, a reason a man can wrap his hands around and control. *There has got to be a reason.*' But the evidence for that is not strong. His luck and his friends' ill-luck seem cut from the same cloth. Desperately needing to believe in some compensatory mechanism which will provide evidence for an underlying principle of justice, he convinces himself that the child which was to provide meaning for his life will be born dead and that this will expiate the curse of good fortune. When it proves healthy he transfers his sense of despair to the baby, refusing to embrace it as a symbol of his fate. But where, in the novel, this had deepened into paranoia and psychosis, here he is pulled back from the brink by his wife. When he could prevent the poisoning of the mink he has been raising for the fur trade (a fate to which his neighbour's animals had already succumbed), his wife intervenes. Only by allowing them to die will he recognize his own control over events. In a speech that has echoes of *The Golden Years*, she insists that 'You are the god now; there was nothing in the sky that gave you things, nothing that could take them away! It was always you . . . ' Frieber ends by preparing to embrace the child he had rejected, thereby assuming responsibility for what he has created.

The paradox is that the consistency with which all but David's hopes are blighted and dreams denied almost amounts to a coherent order. Shory's cynicism seems validated by what emerges as the governing principle of novel and play alike – irony. In the novel the sheer relentlessness of the disasters is less apparent as the extended narrative provides a fuller context for lives which are not seen simply in terms of their pathology. In the play the irony can seem mannered.

This is in some degree mitigated in the revised version which was produced at the Forest Theatre in New York in November, 1944 and further revised in 1988. The characteristic Miller humour is now given greater space, motivation is strengthened, characters made more plausible. What is essentially a fable about human freedom is now rooted more overtly in the politics of wartime Europe. But most crucially, perhaps, for his future development as a playwright, he stumbled on a dramatically significant realisation about his own characters. 'One day, quite suddenly, I saw that Amos and David were brothers and Pat their father. There was a different anguish in the story now, an indescribably new certainty that I could speak from deep within myself. I had seen something no one else had ever seen.' Thus David Frieber became David Beeves. It was indeed to prove a crucial insight to Miller, for whom brothers, and their relationship to their father, were to be at the centre of *All My Sons*, *Death of a Salesman* and *The Price*. It was not simply that two parts of the play which otherwise had been thematically but not psychologically linked, now came together, but that here, as in the later plays, abstract concerns could be earthed in living relationships. And here, as in *Death of a Salesman* and *The Price* (and even his adaptation of Ibsen's *An Enemy of the People*), the two brothers represent differing approaches to experience, apparent success and apparent failure, the material and the spiritual.

The father/son relationship also implicitly raises questions about the meaning of individual lives, the degree to which unrealised dreams can simply be displaced, deferred, a psychologically credible curse handed from generation to generation. So, Patterson Beeves, who had convinced his son of the inevitability of his success as a baseball player –

a success that renders his school work irrelevant – becomes linked to him by a blend of love and guilt when that dream collapses in exactly the same way that Willy Loman was to be tied to his own son, Biff, whose success at football was to have expiated his father's sense of failure.

The Man Who Had All The Luck has a double context: the Depression and the war. Miller himself has said that though it 'hardly seemed a Depression story . . . it was, with its obsessive terror of failure and its guilt for success.' But, more than that, the Depression seemed to destroy a certain faith in natural order. The arbitrariness with which livelihoods were lost, lives ruined or, occasionally, fortunes made, seemed to suggest a social system without logic and a moral system with neither sanction nor foundation. Indeed the very word 'system' now seemed without meaning. As Miller himself remarked, 'Until 1929 I thought things were pretty solid. Specifically, I thought – like most Americans – that somebody was in charge. I didn't know who it was, but it was probably a businessman, and he was a realist, a no-nonsense fellow, practical, honest, responsible. In 1929 he jumped out of a window. It was bewildering.' The logic seemed to have gone out of experience. As David Beeves remarks, when confronted with accumulating evidence for the arbitrariness of events: 'The world is a madhouse. What can you build in a madhouse that won't be knocked down when you turn your back?' After a decade of Depression, the despair voiced by so many of the play's characters could be seen as having a clear social foundation.

It also had a clear political foundation. Begun shortly after the completion of *The Golden Years*, it reflects that play's concern with a collapse of will that had an immediate political correlative. So it is that Miller has said that, 'The fear of drift, more exactly a drift into some kind of fascism, lay hidden somewhere in the origins of *The Man Who Had All The Luck* . . . seemingly a genre piece about mid-

America that has no connection with any of these political questions.' The characters in this play feel the helpless victims of circumstance, unable to intervene in their own lives, unable to deflect events, to seize their own fate. They thereby conspire in the idea of their own impotence. Since the period during which he wrote the novel and at least two versions of the play coincided with the appeasement of Chamberlain and the collapse of European democracies in the face of the seeming implacability and absolutism of fascism, it is certainly tempting to see novel and play as something other than a contemplation of abstract issues having to do with human freedom or determinism. A key speech, indeed, is added to the revised version, a speech in which Gus, (now Austrian rather than German), insists that a man must believe that 'on this earth he is the boss of his life. Not the leafs – the teacups, not the stars. In Europe I have seen already millions of Davids walking around, millions. They gave up already . . . ' The conclusion that he draws is the need for compassion and commitment, a revived humanism. The conclusion drawn by David (until his wife forces him to reassess his life) is that he lives in an absurd world. But, as with *The Golden Years*, the political and the metaphysical co-exist.

What is at stake in *The Man Who Had All The Luck* is what was to be at stake in most of Miller's drama – the question of the individual's responsibility for his own actions, the extent to which we are the authors not only of our own fate but our own identities. His characters are all too willing to deny that responsibility, failing to recognize in the self the generator of action and values, as of betrayal and denial. So it is that Joe Killer, in *All My Sons*, was to cite family responsibility, Willy Loman, in *Death of a Salesman*, a threatening modernity, the judges in *The Crucible* civic duty, and Eddie Carbone in *A View from the Bridge*, natural justice as a justification for their betrayals. But the thrust of all of his work is to insist on causality, to show the degree to which the individual is responsible for his actions. *The Man Who Had All The Luck* edges towards the position ultimately identified in *After the Fall* in which the protagonist, Quentin, finally comes to acknowledge that there is no judge on the bench, no god in the sky, no one but himself, totally abandoned and hence totally responsible. And if David Beeves also arrives at what is a familiar American existentialism – part of a national myth of self-invention – this conviction is hard-won, requiring, as it does, that he disburden himself of all his property and confront an absurdity which need not be disabling, provided only that he acknowledge the burden of responsibility that he will be assuming in return.

The sense of order that David Beeves had looked for in life exists not in the structure of existence but in the mind and imagination of the individual and, as Miller would later insist, in the shaping power of art:

> One had the right to write because other people needed news of the inner world, and if they went too long without such news they would go mad with the chaos of their lives. With the greatest of presumption I conceived that the great writer was the destroyer of chaos, a man privy to the councils of the hidden gods who administer the hidden laws that bind us all and destroy us if we do not know them. And chaos, for one thing, was life lived oblivious of history. As time went on, a lot of time, it became clear to me that I was not only reporting to others but to myself first and foremost. I wrote not only to find a way into the world but to hold it away from me so that it would not devour me.

The hidden gods are not, as David had come to believe, external to the self. To Miller, here, as in the later plays, the crucial discovery is that they are indeed part of an 'inner world' in which imagination and will combine to generate an order created rather than discovered. The secret of history lies in the fact of causality, a logic that binds the individual to his actions and actions to their consequences. As he has said more than once, a central theme of his work – a theme which lies at the heart of this early play – is that the chickens come home to roost. That is both the burden his characters have to bear and the source of their hope. The tension between the given and the willed is the essence of that tragic spirit which then, and later, he determined to capture.

The two plays in this volume take us back nearly fifty years, to the very beginning of a career that has been one of the most distinguished in American dramatic history. The surprise is not that they reveal the occasional weakness – the purple prose of *The Golden Years*, the contrivances, in the early version, of plot and character in *The Man Who Had All The Luck* – but that they show a writer who, so early in his career, chose to regard the theatre as a legitimate arena for social, political and moral debate and who, in doing so, created a drama in which such public issues were rooted in private anxieties. Here, as later, he is fascinated by the person who is so committed to an idea, an interpretation of experience, a belief, that he is prepared to risk everything, no matter how misguided that commitment might be. Montezuma and David Beeves, no less than Willy Loman, John Proctor and Eddie Carbone, are determined, finally, to discover in their own actions a meaning and an identity which they had once sought elsewhere. None will settle for half measures no matter how fatally illusioned they may be. All but Beeves go to their deaths and even he was only reprieved in the play version, not the novel. Perhaps when Miller was writing in the war years, for wartime production, the irony of a man's discovering his power over his own life only in the act of taking it was too clear a glimpse of the absurd to be sustained.

There are moments in *The Golden Years* when the poetry

rings out with a clarity and a force to match anything in *The Crucible*; moments in *The Man Who Had All The Luck* – such as that in which we witness the dying hopes of a would-be baseball player – when we are watching a master story teller who was, indeed, at that very moment poised between two possible careers, that of the novelist and the dramatist. We have the evidence of his novel, *Focus*, and of his short stories, that both careers were equally plausible. Already, in these two early plays, however, we can begin to see the loss that would have been suffered by the American theatre had his talents been deflected into other paths.

CHRISTOPHER BIGSBY

Methuen Modern Plays

include work by

Jean Anouilh
John Arden
Margaretta D'Arcy
Wolfgang Bauer
Brendan Behan
Edward Bond
Bertolt Brecht
Howard Brenton
Mikhail Bulgakov
Caryl Churchill
Noël Coward
Sarah Daniels
Shelagh Delaney
David Edgar
Rainer Werner Fassbinder
Michael Frayn
Dario Fo
Max Frisch
Simon Gray
Peter Handke
Vaclav Havel
Kaufman & Hart
Barrie Keeffe
Arthur Kopit
Larry Kramer
Franz Xaver Kroetz
Stephen Lowe
John McGrath
David Mamet
David Mercer
Arthur Miller
Mtwa, Ngema & Simon
Peter Nichols
Joe Orton
Louise Page
Harold Pinter
Luigi Pirandello
Stephen Poliakoff
David Rudkin
Willy Russell
Jean-Paul Sartre
Wole Soyinka
C. P. Taylor
Theatre Workshop
Peter Whelan
Nigel Williams
Victoria Wood